GROWING UP HEALTHY IN A WORLD OF DIGITAL MEDIA

A guide for parents and caregivers
of children and adolescents

First published in German as
Gesund aufwachsen in der digitalen Medienwelt
by **diagnose:media**, Stuttgart, Germany
kontakt@diagnose-media.org   www.diagnose-media.org

English translation by Astrid Klee
Richard Brinton, Neal Carter, Michaela Glöckler and Patrice Maynard, editors

First English edition published April 2019
InterActions
37 Chandos Road, Stroud, GL5 3QT, UK
interactionspublishing@outlook.com

Second English edition published September 2019
Waldorf Publications
351 Fairview Avenue, Suite 625
Hudson, NY 12534

ISBN #978-1-943582-35-8
© 2019 Waldorf Publications

All rights reserved. No part of this publication may be reproduced, stored in a retrieval system or transmitted in any form or by any means without the prior permission of the publisher.

GROWING UP HEALTHY
IN A WORLD OF DIGITAL MEDIA

A guide for parents and caregivers
of children and adolescents

Contents

Preface to the original German edition 6

Preface to the English edition 7

Introduction 8

1. **Why this guide?** 10
   1.1 Media education aligned with childhood development
   1.2 Strengthen your child's experiences in the real world!
   1.3 How we as parents provide guidance

2. **Protecting children from mobile electromagnetic (EM) radiation – from the beginning! What we should take seriously** 30
   2.1 The biological effects of mobile radiation
   2.2 Precautions and recommendations

3. **Early childhood (0–3 years)**
   Without screen media and without irradiating children's toys! 44
   3.1 What do young children need for their healthy development?
   3.2 Screen media has a different effect on children
   3.3 Responsible media education during early childhood

4. **Nursery school age (4–6 years)**
   Real world experience and movement – as much as possible! 54
   4.1 What do children need for their healthy development?
   4.2 This is the effect of screen media at nursery school age
   4.3 Responsible media education at nursery school age

5. **The first years of school (6–9 years)**
   Supervise and limit the use of screen media! 62
   5.1 Developmental steps in the primary school years
   5.2 Psychologists and pediatricians describe the fundamental needs of children
   5.3 Responsible media education at primary school age

6. From childhood to adolescence (10–16 years)
On the path to media maturity 70
6.1 What do adolescents need for their healthy development?
6.2 The impact of screen media
6.3 Growing into mature and healthy media usage
6.4 Long-term learning with new media
6.5 Security software and technical support

7. The dangers of using digital media 86
7.1 Stress associated with social media
7.2 Excessive media use and the dangers of addiction
7.3 Careless approach to private information
7.4 Cyberbullying and internet harassment
7.5 Sites on the net which are unsuitable for adolescents

8. Internet and the law – information for parents 126
8.1 The right of informational self-determination
8.2 Internet criminal law and the Youth Protection Act
8.3 Copyright law
8.4 Purchase agreements and liability on the internet
8.5 Legal obligations of parents

Bibliography and References 140

Partners/Sponsors 153

Acknowledgments 156

Preface to the original German edition

Growing up healthy in a world of digital media is an initiative for the promotion of competent and age-appropriate use of digital media by children and adolescents – for the support of parents, schools and other people affected, and for networking with experts and specialist institutions.

The new digital media of information and communications technology (ICT), such as smartphones, tablets, notebooks and games consoles, all take up ever more space in the lives of children and adolescents. Currently young people are increasingly overwhelmed by the new media, as is evident to parents and teachers. Many observations and studies show that premature contact with the new media by children and adolescents is associated with considerable risks to their development and health.

The goal of the initiative, on the one hand, is to clarify the dangers and risks of the new media, and on the other hand, to illustrate protective measures and opportunities for action, to either avoid the dangers completely or be able to approach them appropriately. At the core of the debate are the psychological aspects, communication behavior, the potential for addiction, safeguarding the private sphere and the negative health impacts due to continuous irradiation from the use of wireless communication.

In the sphere of psycho-social risks especially, the discussion about appropriate educational uses is already well underway and by no means concluded. The initiatives in this guidebook aim to present an educational standpoint which represents an appropriate balance between the needs of children and adolescents and the restrictions which are required as precautionary measures to safeguard against the inherent dangers.

www.diagnose-media.org
Partner and sponsor for the initiative

Preface to the English edition

The commercialization of childhood has already been a heightened issue for the past several decades. The proliferation of televisions in the 1950s and 1960s, then small electronic games and toys in the 1970s and 1980s increased the attractions for children. But it was really only in the 1990s with the miniaturization of computers, enabling interactive video games and other devices to be held in the hand, that the capturing of children's attention took on new dimensions. Technology firms realized the huge potential. In his marketing book, *Kids as Consumers,* published in 1992, James McNeal wrote that kids "are in a perfect position to be taken." Marketing strategies were outlined to bypass parents.

The capturing of children's attention took off in further exponential proportions with the advent of the smartphone in 2007, giving users internet connection wherever they were. For families this has posed enormous problems, with half of parents in one survey saying that smartphones have become the number one issue in the home, with technology firms designing products for maximum addiction potential. Netflix CEO Reed Hastings said they were now "competing with sleep." Company lobbying has influenced government programs for computers in nurseries, despite there being no evidence to support this as a helpful or healthy addition, and with much evidence to the contrary. A large OECD study in 2015 of 70 countries even questioned the benefits of computers in education in general.

In the past few years there has been a new awakening. Questions are being raised about the appropriateness of media technology in childhood. Already several years ago one survey noted that 90% of people thought it's not right how marketing people try to buy children, yet only 7% felt able to do something. How can we take steps to protect our children?

This book fills a gap, describing the important developmental phases in childhood which have a bearing on the introduction of media technology, giving practical tips for parents on how to work with it in family life in a safe way. It acknowledges not everybody will be able to follow the same approach, yet shows how we can think through step by step what is for the benefit and well-being of the child and young person in our care. We are glad to have been part of the effort to bring this informative book to the English speaking world.

Richard Brinton, InterActions

Introduction

Hardly a day passes that one does not hear or read something topical on the theme of digitization. It is foreseen that in the next 20 years, 60-70% of current professions will be replaced by electronic devices and robots. It is no wonder that many parents think: This is the world children are growing up in – why should they not also, from the start, be confronted by this technology and get used to it, with the motto: Early practice makes perfect? Additionally, official educational policies are heading precisely in this direction.

What is overlooked here is that technology operated by human consciousness also very strongly influences its development. This is not a problem for older adolescents and adults, if their brains had the opportunity of developing healthily in an analogue (i.e., real) world – however, for those youths where this process has not yet been concluded, it is a different matter. As a result there increasingly are warning voices, especially from the spheres of science, medicine and developmental psychology.

Research results from many studies and from large meta-analyses have been presented which indicate the side-effects and dangers from premature digitization in nursery schools and schools: impairment of frontal lobe development and the related autonomous thought and control capabilities, postural and eye damage, loss of empathy, deficiencies in verbal powers of expression, dependence on social networks, the danger of addiction – not to mention the side-effects, not considered nearly enough yet, of electro-smog on the nervous system which in childhood and adolescence still reacts much more sensitively than later on.

Then it should also be considered that prominent IT greats such as Steve Jobs, Bill Gates and Jeff Bezos did not allow their children access to smartphones and that, according to statistics, the children of academics spend far less time in front of a screen than the rest of the population. Developmental neurologists such as Prof. Hüther and economic experts such as McAfee, director of Digital Business at the Massachusetts Institute of Technology (MIT) in Cambridge, agree that in a future world determined by information technology, what is needed above all is creativity, social competence, as well as an ability to think and act entrepreneurially.

In fact, the Chinese entrepreneur Jack Ma who created Alibaba, the Asian Amazon competitor, cut to the chase when he said at a world economic forum in Davos: Instead of cramming knowledge, which after all every computer gives you access to at the press of a button, schools should teach "values, trust, independent thinking, teamwork," and give more space to creative subjects such as art, culture, music and sports. These creative and entrepreneurial competencies, however, have their developmental foundation in the real world, not in the digital world! We have to consider this paradox – social skills, creativity and imaginative thinking require for their development direct interaction with people and discussions with others who think differently, not with a computer. What is the solution?

All this knowledge does not help us to master everyday family life, in which the smartphone has not only become an indispensable accompaniment, but often also a bone of contention. What is needed is clear information and practical tips for guiding children and adolescents at their respective ages so as to avoid the possible damages. That is the goal of this media guidebook. It illustrates what children and adolescents require to gain healthy entry into an age of media technology.

This book offers perspectives from many experts and organizations – media experts and educators – as can be seen from the list of supporters and sponsors of this guidebook. What unites them is their love for young people and the great responsibility we have toward them. Our hope is that as many children and adolescents as possible can grow up healthily, so that they can manage their digital future competently and that they will be up to the task of facing the demands they will encounter in life.

Dornach, Switzerland, September 2018
Michaela Glöckler, MD

Why this guide?

1.1 Media education aligned with childhood development

"Children mostly know what they want, however, they often do not know what they need."

Jesper Juul, Danish family therapist

Does this sound familiar?
When children are little: With the television or tablet switched on – our children are immediately fascinated and quiet.

We can
- complete our work
- take a deep breath and relax
- take long car trips with the family without stress
- avoid being constantly irritated by wishes and needs…

Then when the children are older: always on the mobile phone!
- Can't you help in the kitchen for a change? – Not now!
- When are you finally going to do your homework? – Later!
- Are you still awake – it is already after 11? – So what?
- Can't you put away your mobile phone while we eat? – Hmm, what?

But maybe this also sounds familiar?
- The child can play with things (from the real world) for a long time;
- can build up his or her own fantasy world and creatively invent new things,
- is sociable and gets along well with other children – is "team-minded."

Children should only later engage competently and responsibly with digital technology and future "new" media – not at the same time as adults around them. That is the aim of this guide – and, of course, of us all. Parents might ask: How is this goal achieved? And can this goal be reached even as children are called to come into contact with digital media as early as possible to learn to use its potential when very young – a goal currently and constantly proclaimed?

This guide will try to navigate you through the discussion of these questions. The starting point for this is the overriding question:

What do children and adolescents need for healthy development?
Studies show that healthy (brain) development is the best guarantee for the ability to use digital media competently and responsibly, in children, adolescents and adults. The question is thus: Can digital media promote healthy brain development or has it been proven to be detrimental or even dangerous?

Educators, pediatricians and media experts warn
Today we know that, especially in the first years of life, screen media can play a calamitous role, as it has an increasingly inhibiting role developmentally the more it is used (see chapters 2, 3 and 4).

Toddlers already display the first signs of addiction-like behavior. In addition, disturbances in brain development can easily occur, with dire consequences.

Even older children, who increasingly spend more time on screen devices, are in danger, as is shown by the topical BLIKK-media study of 2017[1]: More frequent media consumption can lead to speech inhibition, attention deficiency, concentration and sleep disturbances, hyperactivity, aggression, right through to reading and spelling disturbances.

Children and adolescents are only from their twelfth year – gradually introduced in moderation – able to start using screen media independently and appropriately.

If age restrictions for driving, cigarette and alcohol consumption are applied, then currently there are many factors which speak in favor of applying restrictions to the use of digital network media!

What do developmental psychology and neurobiology say?
Developmental psychology and neurobiology have long ago researched the requirements for healthy brain development in children: The development of children's senses, and especially of the brain, is all the more enhanced the more the childhood years are filled with movement activities – running, climbing, somersaulting, balancing, and much more – and the more intensively the child is exposed to the real things of the natural environment, with fellow human beings, animals and plants.

The maturation and increasing differentiation of the neural networks in the frontal lobe (cortex) is an ongoing process for more than two decades: At stake is learning to write, calculate and read, which in turn enables new memory content and allows more differentiated mental activity to emerge.

For healthy brain development, at every age the child has to undergo characteristic processes and develop corresponding abilities, which is illustrated in the following chapters. Decisive at every developmental stage is the question whether the child's inner maturity is ready to meet the demands of using media, with all of its appealing possibilities, or whether it provokes disturbances or even causes damage.

Media education should thus be guided by the developmental stage of children and adolescents!

For childhood this means (see section 1.2):

"'A childhood without computers is the best start for a digital world!'

This thesis of Gerald Lembke and Ingo Leipner[2] is not at all paradoxical: If you reduce the impact of digital media on children and instead allow them to move a lot and enjoy nature, and to handle analogue [i.e., real] things, you are promoting (!) brain development, because adolescents and adults later need high cognitive abilities to master the challenges of digital media."

Teuchert-Noodt 2016, see reading suggestion on page 17

Early media use is short-sighted and risky

The very early use of media within the family and school is thus short-sighted, highly risky and counter-productive: It is not based on the findings of educational and neuro-biological science. The widespread opinion that "if you do not introduce media to your child at a young enough age, you are obstructing his or her future" is a disastrous mistake.

This viewpoint is based uncritically on the claims of the media industry and its marketing interests, which markets the early use of media using concepts of progress which are pushed through to the ministries with the help of lobby groups: "Boundless hopes are stoked to ensure that digital products pervade our everyday life."[2]

It seems paradoxical, but according to scientific findings:

The consumption of media too early in life hinders the development of exactly the key concepts which are later needed for the mature mastery of digital media.

Suggested reading

Sue Palmer (2016)
Upstart: The Case for Raising the School Starting Age and Providing What the Under-sevens Really Need, Floris Books

Susan Greenfield (2014)
Mind Change – How Digital Technologies Are Leaving Their Mark on Our Brains, Random House

Interview with Gertraud Teuchert-Noodt (2017)
Digital Media Are a Great Danger for Our Brain,
visionsblog.info/en/2017/05/20/digital-media-great-danger-brain
(orig. German article, Umwelt, Medizin, Gesellschaft, pp28–32)

1.2 Strengthen your child's experiences in the real world!

This is what we as parents wish for our children: Our children should learn to handle both real world and digital media competently and with an awareness of the risks. But which developmental steps does a person have to have undergone to be able to operate digital devices independently and confidently?

And what can we as parents do, so that we do not "sow" something in our children now which we later do not wish to "harvest" in our adolescents (see page 12 and page 95 ff)?

Coping in the real world is essential for coping in a virtual world

The new screen media do not appear in the lives of our children instead of television and videos, but additionally, and increase the time they sit in front of a screen. This leads to an increased displacement of experiences in the real world, with the virtual world increasingly replacing the real world.

However, children have to complete their physical and emotional developmental steps in the real world: This includes speech development, the development of gross and fine motor skills, the sharpening of all the senses, testing and exploration of things and processes in the real world, learning the rules of social interaction and much more. It is thus generally true: The use of media quickly becomes a problem when the child no longer has enough time for his or her biologically necessary developmental steps in the real world.

An example: If your child does not experience enough social interaction with other children, which e.g., allows him or her to learn to perceive the needs of others and to consider them, then social developmental deficiencies, e.g., lack of empathy, can arise.

On the other hand: If, e.g., your child in social interaction with other children feels constantly rejected and feels that his or her needs are not considered, then communication with virtual friends over Facebook, WhatsApp & co. can be perceived as an adequate replacement. This can mean that the consumption of media increases.

Or if children cannot often enough undertake or try out something with their friends or parents, then there is a big danger that they will try to fulfill their wishes through virtual action games or role playing games on the PC or tablet. In the end these are futile and unhealthy attempts of a child to meet his or her needs and to master necessary developmental steps. The use of media can quickly become a problem, which means: The consumption of media gets out of hand.

This behavior is further reinforced by the addictive potential that is inherent in many of the digital screen media apps. Children need, first and foremost, to find their way in the real world, physically and emotionally, which in any case always remains the primary life determining world.

We now know: Only once the child has mastered his or her biologically necessary developmental stages at the different ages, can he or she develop the ability to competently and meaningfully manage media.

What is important?
Mainly, it is important to provide children with a variety of opportunities to test their senses, to move their bodies, to explore nature, to communicate with their fellow humans, in other words, to "conquer" the real world. If your child has a hobby, e.g., likes playing football or is learning to play an instrument or likes to build or craft something, then a smartphone is not so important because during this time it is not used at all or is used only as an aid (e.g.,

for taking pictures). This creates a counter-balance to the virtual world and protects your child in a natural way from its risks. It is therefore important that parents try to create enthusiasm in their children for activities in the real world. This is the best foundation for the development of media maturity in adolescence.

Ever younger use of digital media, on the other hand, hinders exactly what children need to learn and what we wish as parents. Children should thus be protected from the virtual world, rather than exposing them to it too early. This was already clearly recognized by Bill Gates and Steve Jobs, founders of Microsoft and Apple, as well as other IT bosses: Their children received smartphones only when they turned 14. See: www.nytimes.com/2014/09/11/fashion/steve-jobs-apple-was-a-low-tech-parent.html?_r=0 and www.weforum.org/agenda/2017/10/why-gates-and-jobs-shielded-their-kids-from-tech.

In the use of media, agreements and rules for children and adults are helpful and decisive
A lot of research and scientific studies show: If parents accept the use of media by their children without reservations, and do not restrict and control it, they are faced with significant behavioral and health risks for their children and adolescents. This strains and weakens the family, as well as the whole of society (see chapters 3 and 7). The ability to restrict oneself and to put cravings on hold is still developing in adolescents. Putting in place boundaries and coming to agreements are thus necessary safeguards for your children.

Parents should especially not enable or allow toddlers any use at all. Ideally children should grow up without a smartphone, tablet or PC until the age of 12 years. They should first develop a strong competence in relation to the real world around them.

There is no doubt: We cannot withhold digital media from our children and adolescents and cannot leave them alone with the influences and changes which they bring about. They are constantly exposed to the temptations of digital screen media through the media and especially through their friends. If you decide to buy your child a smartphone or a tablet, then your child will be exposed to risks which should be taken seriously.

It is then responsible to protect your child as much as possible by placing boundaries early on, i.e., clear rules as to how long computer, tablet and smartphone may be used per day, if at all (details can be found in sections 4.3, 5.3 and 6.3). This requires from you a good sense of empathy about the developmental level of your child and enormous skills in parenting. However, it also depends on your example, as is explained in section 1.3 in more detail.

"Essentially it means setting boundaries, taking a stand. It means having a clear vision and to uphold it. With loving consequences, praise and encouragement. In constant discussion with oneself and with one's children."

Katharina Saalfrank (2006)[33]

Boundaries are often set too late
To only set limits when the internet consumption of the child is already out of hand and stretches well beyond reasonable times inevitably leads to difficult confrontations with the child. It also does not guarantee that they can be enforced and that the child gets a handle on his or her internet consumption.

Many educators are in agreement: Children want boundaries and rules in good time (!). They want clarity, they want to know where they stand. Boundaries give children structure, stability and security, but also elicit discussion. A lack of boundaries on the other hand causes insecurity and cause a lack of stability and restraint in children. Even the youngest ones need boundaries and even a baby understands the underlying rules from the reactions of the parents (see suggested reading on page 25).

Setting boundaries – there is no formula
It is the task of the parents to decide what is important to them, which boundaries make sense and how they want to apply them. If children understand in good time what is acceptable and what is not, there will be fewer arguments later and it will be self-evident for the children. However, boundaries in family life may prove to be unsuitable and must therefore be re-established continually, especially as children grow older.

The setting of boundaries is a process which depends on the age of the child, and especially considers what is needed at this moment in the youngster's development; what the child wishes to have should be subordinate to this.

In this way children will be able to better develop an autonomous and healthy use of digital media and will be largely protected from the risks of digital media.

What do the experts recommend? The 3-6-9-12 rule

The French psychologist Serge Tisseron has formulated typical stages of development and corresponding recommendations for media usage, which parents can use as an initial guide in media education, for the age groups up to 3 years, from 3 to 6 years, from 6 to 9 years, from 9 to 12 years and from 12 years onward, (see www.3-6-9-12.org, or healthnwellness.co.uk/children-and-screen-time-the-3-6-9-12-rule-you-need-to-know/ for English summary).

This guide in many respects follows the recommendations of Tisseron, among others the suggestion that until 12 years the parents alone determine the rules regarding media usage. Joint agreements should only be made with the child after that.

Serge Tisseron

Boundaries and rules are a compromise

Growing up without any digital media, and thus without its risks, would be best, especially for children up to the age of 12 years. This is clearly supported by scientific findings; however, it is not given much consideration in political decision making.

If you cannot manage to withstand current trends and societal pressure on the family, you may have to give in partially and decide on a compromise.

All recommendations about media usage in this guide book are therefore an expression of perhaps a reasonable middle way and are to be understood as a fallback option. Nevertheless, this is clear: From a scientific point of view you are not protecting your child from the risks to his or her health and biological development!

Suggested reading

Save Childhood Movement
Manifesto for the Early Years: Putting Children First.
Available as a PDF document:
www.savechildhood.net/wp-content/uploads/2016/10/PUTTING-CHILDREN-FIRST.pdf

Lou Harvey-Zahra (2016)
Happy Child, Happy Home: Conscious Parenting and Creative Discipline, Floris Books
(See Chapter 7, What's stopping play today? and other chapters for creative alternatives)

Aric Sigman (2019)
A Movement for Movement – Screen Time, Physical Activity and Sleep: A New Integrated Approach for Children
Available as a PDF document:
www.api-play.org/wp-content/uploads/sites/4/2019/01/API-Report-A-Movement-for-Movement-A4FINALWeb.pdf

Myla and Jon Kabat-Zinn (2014)
Everyday Blessings: Mindfulness for Parents, Piatkus
(See Chapter 6 on Media Madness)

1.3 How we as parents provide guidance

*"There is no use in bringing up children –
they will copy everything you do anyway!"*

Unknown

Parents are the example
Parents are the example for their children. The example that parents set for their children forms their mode of behavior, attitudes and feelings. Your example forms your children more than any formative measures: It can thus significantly support or hinder your child's healthy development (Saalfrank 2006[33]).

It is therefore important that especially you as parent are not constantly absorbed by a smartphone or the internet, thereby having less and less time for your children.

Be conscious of devoting your attention totally to your children when you are with them (see image). A smartphone (or tablet) is disruptive! The more you speak and communicate non-verbally with your children, the better your children's speech ability, thinking and feeling develop. During communal mealtimes at the table, screen media should be taboo for all family members.

Parents can easily record their own media habits. There are Apps for recording and managing screen usage behavior, e.g., for a smartphone:

- SPACE App, formerly Breakfree
- Menthal App (menthal.org)
- 'Screen Time' and App Limits features as part of Apple's new iOS12 phones
  For a comprehensive listing of 'Screen Time Management Apps' see: www.screenagersmovie.com/parenting-apps/

Parents are guides and supporters
Don't only be an example. Also be interested in what your children are doing on the screen: For example, in the games they are engaged with. Take the time to discover and experience what media has to offer, together with your children: Then you can talk about what you have found, elaborate on it and explain what your children do not yet understand.

This can have a very positive effect on the parent-child relationship. Discussions are opportunities to convey your own evaluation of the quality and content of what has been experienced.

Adolescents need support, and parents can, e.g., enable balance in the real world (by means of communal activities) or discuss fundamental questions with them: How indispensible are mobile phone, etc., really? How would life be if there was no smartphone or tablet or if it was not constantly being used? Can we try this for a while?

Suggested reading

Dr. Elizabeth Kilbey (2017)
Unplugged Parenting: How to Raise Happy, Healthy Children in the Digital Age, Headline Home

Edmond Schoorel (2016)
Managing Screen Time – Raising Balanced Children in the Digital Age, Floris Books

Sue Palmer (2006)
Toxic Childhood – How the Modern World Is Damaging Our Children and What We Can Do about It, Orion

Jesper Juul (2006)
No! The Art of Saying No! with a Clear Cconscience, AuthorHouse

Parents are the media custodians

Parents need to be informed about the different technical possibilities of digital devices (smartphone, tablet, router, PC, etc.). However, more important is the question: Are these devices suitable for children? What can be done about this? If these devices are already being used by your children, then the positioning of technical devices (not in the child's room), the activation of filter software or the installation of child safety programs, and so forth (see section 6.5) are of great importance if you want to protect your child from the risks.

Many of the risks in the use of digital media have meanwhile become commonly known (see chapters 2 and 7). A discussion with your children or adolescents about these risks and how they can be avoided is necessary.

Regulations on the protection of children and young people are different in every country. In Germany there is the Youth Protection Act. (the JuSchG – see www.t1p.de/uyan). It states:

Even if children or adolescents under 16 years have been given a mobile or smartphone by parents/grandparents/... as "gifts," the parents carry the responsibility for what the children do with their smartphones. Correspondingly, they have the right, and in principle also the duty, of controlling the activities of their children or adolescents.

Further discussion of regulations is in chapters 7 and 8, with indicators for finding those for the country you are in.

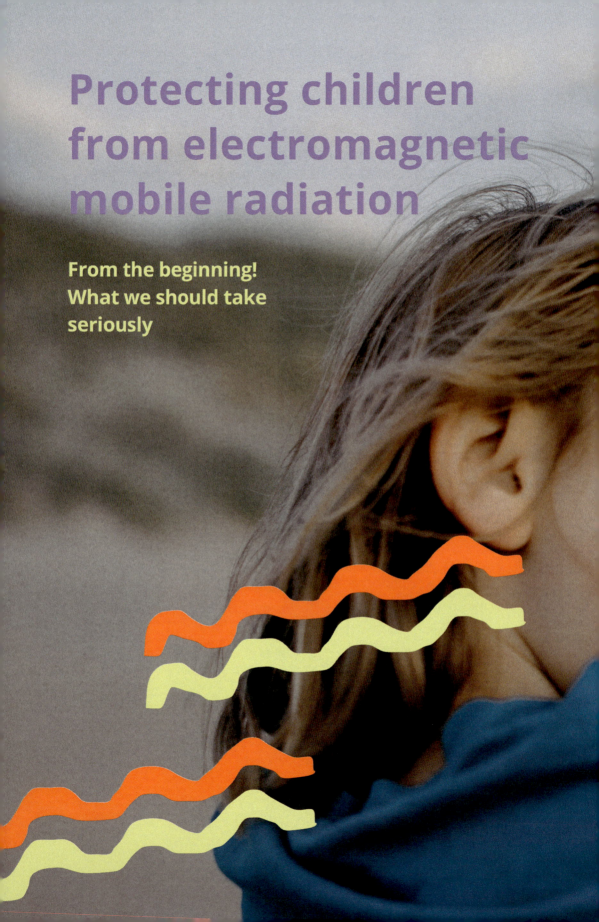

Protecting children from electromagnetic mobile radiation

From the beginning! What we should take seriously

CHAPTER 2   PROTECTING CHILDREN FROM ELECTROMAGNETIC MOBILE RADIATION

2.1 The biological effects of mobile radiation

More than 40 years of intensive research has shown that even exposure to electromagnetic radiation below safety limits is associated with significant risks for the health of people, as well as for the health of animals and plants.

Damage to health from EM radiation
The health risks associated with the effects of radiation are often under estimated or even ignored. Scientific studies are providing ever clearer proof: Especially continual radiation below safety limits, which many people are exposed to as a result of the steady increase of radiation devices (e.g., Wi-Fi, Bluetooth, UMTS, etc.), is a major source of health risks. To what extent these risks have already become a reality, is shown by the annual statistics of health insurance companies.[3][4]

The behavioral risks accompanying smartphones, etc., are negatively increased especially in children and adolescents as a result of the health dangers of mobile communications radiation. As a result, children already display decreased performance capacity at school.

Warnings worldwide even from the mobile communications industry

For years already, international appeals from doctors, scientific, medical and environmental organizations, the European Union, the European Parliament and many other institutions have been warning about the health risks of mobile radiation and have been demanding a reduction of radiation and urgent protective measures for children and adolescents. The German Federal Office for Radiation Protection (Bundesamt für Strahlenschutz) in its recommendations confirms that a health risk cannot be precluded:[5]

- *Rather use cable connections* if wireless technology can be avoided.
- Avoid the installation of central Wi-Fi access points in the immediate vicinity of places where people often spend time, for example at work.

Meanwhile there are even warnings from the industry itself:

In their safety instructions, manufacturers indicate that their mobile device should be kept at a minimum distance from the body of the user so that the legal safety limits for microwave radiation are not exceeded.

For example, with the smartphone Blackberry Torch 9800, a distance of at least 25mm should be maintained, especially from the abdomen of pregnant women (exposure of the foetus) and adolescents (exposure of the testes). According to the instruction manual for the recent iPhone X, it is recommended: "To reduce exposure to RF energy, use a hands-free option, such as the built-in speakerphone, the supplied headphones, or other similar accessories." Most phone manuals give similar advice.

An instruction manual for Speedport Routers, used by German Telekom, contains the following safety warning:

"The integrated antennae of your Speedport sends and receives radio signals, for example, for the installation of your WLAN. Avoid installing your Speedport in the immediate vicinity of bedrooms, children's rooms and living rooms to minimize, as much as possible, the exposure to electromagnetic fields."

In 2017, the National Frequency Agency (ANFR) of France disclosed that 9 out of 10 of hundreds of mobile phones tested (in 2015) exceeded government radiation limits when in the position they are most often used: in contact with the body. The government had refused to disclose these test results until pressured through court actions. (see ehtrust.org, searching on their website for "ANFR" or "Phonegate")

In many countries (in France, Belgium, Israel, among others) these warnings have already resulted in various legal regulations for the safety of children (see suggested reading at the end of this chapter).

Short-term effects

The short-term biological effects of mobile communications radiation are evident in many children and adolescents especially in

- (increasing and continuous) headaches, tiredness and exhaustion, disturbances in sleep or falling asleep
- agitation, irritability, nervousness, depressive tendencies
- memory and concentration disturbances, dizziness and buzzing in the ears
- learning and behavioral disturbances
- heart and circulatory disturbances (racing heart), to some extent also auditory and visual disturbances

The effects (so-called microwave syndrome) have been confirmed by numerous studies: e.g., a Munich study of 2008 determined that 9% of the underage participants – which for Germany is a good one million children and adolescents – feel affected by mobile communications radiation.

In 2016 a study for a health insurance company for the road construction industry (BKK VBU) demonstrated that almost 74% of grade seven children already regularly suffer from headaches. A recent meta-study was able to show that the headaches increased significantly with increased duration or frequency of use of mobile communications devices.[6]

In many cases the symptoms disappear after a recovery period (at least 2 hours without radiation), but often only when the exposure to radiation stops long-term.

Children have a greater need for protection, as in their case the radiation penetrates much further into the head than in adults (see illustration on this page: Absorption of radiation in the head region according to age[7]).

The child's brain is thus exposed at 3 times the level of an adult, the bones even 10 times more. The nervous and immune systems of children are not yet fully developed and therefore their development is more sensitive to disturbance.

Absorption of radiation in the head region according to age

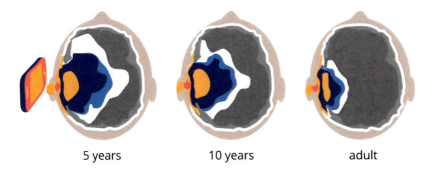

| 5 years | 10 years | adult |

This especially increases the risk of behavioral disturbances. This is proven, in addition to other studies, especially by the results of a WHO study (Divan et al.[8]) with 29,000 children: Children who, while in the womb and/or during early childhood (up to 7 years), were exposed to the radiation of mobile radiation devices (included are also wireless baby monitors) significantly more often developed behavioral problems, including ADHD. This is a clear indication for the causes of the dramatic increase worldwide of children displaying hyperactivity or behavioral problems.

The risk of behavioral disturbances was especially clearly increased (by about 80%), if the mother regularly used a mobile telephone or spent time near radiation sources, or also if the child had used a mobile phone before the age of 7 years. This is because the radiation penetrates the body by a few centimeters and can thus disturb the development of the sensitive foetus.

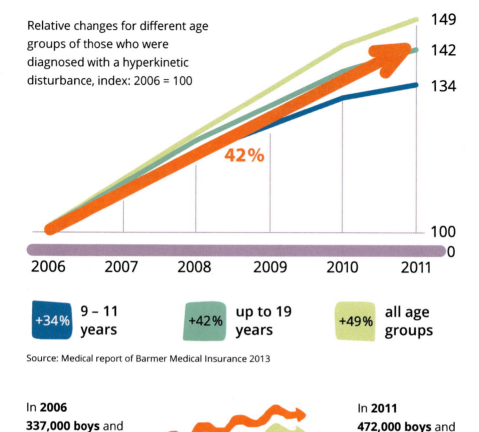

Source: Medical report of Barmer Medical Insurance 2013

In **2006**
337,000 boys and
105,000 girls
were affected

In **2011**
472,000 boys and
149,000 girls
were affected

The Barmer medical report of 2013[4] shows that the risk of behavioral problems as a result of mobile communications radiation has had an impact for a long time already: Within 5 years of the introduction of smartphones, there was a sharp increase in ADHD cases of about 42% in children and adolescents up to the age of 19 (see illustration above). Furthermore, there is evidence that suggests that the risks of miscarriage and deformity are increased.

Long-term effects
The long-term biological effects are, for example, an increased danger of cancer, the negative effect on sperm and fertility, as well as neurological disturbances.

Today we know that for children and adolescents who begin to use mobile telephones before the age of 20, there is an increased risk of malignant brain tumors in later life.

The younger the child is and the longer he or she uses a mobile phone, the more the risk of a tumor increases – up to five times – (Environmental Working Group 2009, Hardell 2009, 2011[8]). Since the introduction of mobile communication in Germany in 1993, the number of children (up to age 15 years) afflicted with cancer continually increases every year (by about 25% in 20 years, Robert Koch Institute 2013). In other countries the developments are even more dramatic.

Cancer in children and adolescents under the age of 20 years has a much shorter latency period (c. 15-20 years) than in adults, which can be up to 40 years. The increased risk of cancer in children and adolescents due to mobile communications radiation can thus have a fatal outcome for the middle phase of their life.

Further information about mobile wireless radiation and its effects can be found on the websites of emf:data and the (German site) diagnose:funk:

www.emfdata.org and www.diagnose-funk.org

2.2 Precautions and recommendations

During pregnancy
- Completely avoid using a mobile or smartphone or other wireless mobile devices such as DECT cordless phones and Wi-Fi supported devices.

- Possibly replace your mobile/smartphone with a landline phone (if possible with an electro-smog reduced receiver, using a Piezo crystal, which can be found on the internet with the search keywords Piezo telephone). If unavoidable, activate your mobile/smartphone only when it is essential and otherwise have it in flight mode (all radiation is switched off).

- Only use a router with Wi-Fi which can be switched off. If possible avoid Wi-Fi in your apartment or only switch it on when necessary and for a short time. Do not make your router available to the public as it then radiates continually!

- Stay away from radiation sources, radiating routers or access points, as well as from people who are using radiating mobile/smartphones/tablets, or ask them to switch their mobiles to flight mode.

After birth

- Avoid using a mobile/smartphone near your child as much as possible! Keep conversations short, and use hands-free equipment. Switch off your mobile/smartphone as often as possible.

- Do not use DECT cordless phones and Wi-Fi. Use radiation free alternatives, such as landlines, wired computers and tablets.

- For baby monitors use only devices which do not hinder or affect biological development, thus no devices using the DECT standard.

- Do not place a switched on mobile in your baby's pushchair.

- If unavoidable, when phoning with a mobile or DECT telephone, keep a distance from other people, especially children.

- Urge your neighbors and also the administration of nursery and primary schools to minimize the exposure of children to radiation.

Children, adolescents and adults

The Vienna medical council published the following recommendations in 2016, which are also supported by many other organizations.

- *Principally the following applies:* Use a mobile/smartphone as little as possible to phone! Minimize your personal exposure to radiation.

- Children under 8 years should not use mobile/smartphones or cordless phones. *Children between 8 and 16 should only use mobile/smartphones in emergencies.*

- At home and in the workplace you should *phone using the landline and only surf via wire connection*: Internet access via a LAN cable does not radiate, is fast and data secure. Continually radiating DECT cordless phones, Wi-Fi access points, data sticks and LTE homebase stations (Box, Cube, etc.) should be avoided! If Wi-Fi is indispensable, then switch it off as often as possible, as it burdens health and is, in the long run, damaging.

- Do not carry your *switched on mobile/smartphone* on your body, not in your trouser pocket (influences later fertility), or in your breast pocket (damages, e.g., breast tissue, heart function and lungs). When not in use store it at a distance from your body, e.g., in your hand bag or school satchel. Use a mobile phone case with radiation protection (e.g., www.healthy-house.co.uk/electro – click on [mobile phone and tablet protection])

- *"Distance is your friend!"* – Preferably never phone with your mobile/smartphone on your ear! Use the built-in hands-free functions or headsets. As a compromise keep it as far from your head as possible or use a mobile phone case with radiation protection.

- Go offline more often and activate *flight mode* as often as possible – for functions such as listening to music, camera, alarm, calculator or offline games it is not necessary to have an internet connection!

- *Fewer Apps means less radiation* – minimize the number of Apps and deactivate the background services on your smartphone which are mostly superfluous. The deactivation of "mobile services" or "data network mode" almost turns your smartphone back into an old fashioned mobile phone: You can still be reached, but avoid much of the unnecessary radiation as a result of the background activity of apps. After activating the apps again you should wait about 5 minutes before using it at all and keep a

distance from the smartphone, as all apps will load missing data at the same time, which can lead to higher radiation exposure.

- *Avoid phoning on a mobile phone* in places with poor reception (basement, lift, bus and train, etc.) – in such situations the mobile phone increases the transmission capacity. *In cases of poor reception* use a headset or, if possible, the hands-free facility!

- When buying a mobile phone, look out for the *lowest possible SAR rate* (see emfacademy.com/cell-phone-radiation-charts-sar-levels-popular-phones/), for OTG capacity (do a search for "OTG phones"), as well as an external aerial terminal! The OTG function (OTG = On The Go), using a USB Ethernet adapter via an USB-OTG cable (e.g., search for keywords USB-OTG-network adaptor) and a network cable especially allow sharing of data from a smartphone or tablet with a cable over the router, thus avoiding Wi-Fi! You will find many instructions also as video if searching for "connect phone to internet with USB-OTG-network adaptor" or similar.

Behavior in the car

- Do not use radiating devices in vehicles (car, bus, train), especially do not phone – without an external antenna the radiation in the vehicle is higher. Besides this, one is distracted while driving and one is disturbing fellow passengers on public transport.

- Many countries have complete bans on the use of SMS or internet usage while driving because the distraction is a danger to oneself and others in traffic.

Further information

There are many websites with further information on research on the effects of EMF radiation as well as products for reducing exposure. A few sites are listed below, but others also exist:

www.emfdata.org/en – the 'diagnose:funk' database 'EMF:data' gives an overview of research in the field of non-ionizing radiation emitted by mobile telephone transceiver stations, mobile phones, smartphones, tablet PCs, wireless network routers, cordless DECT telephones and other devices.

emfacademy.com – a collection of articles with a wealth of information about EMF safety, protection, and resources.

www.procon.org – attempts to provide information and research on the pros and cons of controversial issues, including EMF radiation.

www.healthy-house.co.uk – provides products and advice on a wide range of allergies and sensitivities, including EMF radiation exposure.

Suggested reading

Peter Hensinger, Isabel Wilke (2016)
Wireless Communication Technologies: New Study Findings Confirm Risks of Non-ionizing Radiation, original German in magazine, Umwelt-medizin-gesellschaft 3/2016 (pictured left), available in English as PDF: https://ehtrust.org/wp-content/uploads/Hensinger-Wilke-2016.pdf

Nicolas Pineault (2017)
The Non-Tinfoil Guide to EMFs: How to Fix Our Stupid Use of Technology, CreateSpace Independent Publishing Platform

Internet:

EMF Academy (last update 7 February 2019)
9 Examples of EMF Radiation In Everyday Life (With Solutions)
emfacademy.com/emf-radiation-everyday-life/

Environmental Health Trust
10 Tips To Reduce Cell Phone Radiation
ehtrust.org/take-action/educate-yourself/10-things-you-can-do-to-reduce-the-cancer-risk-from-cell-phones/

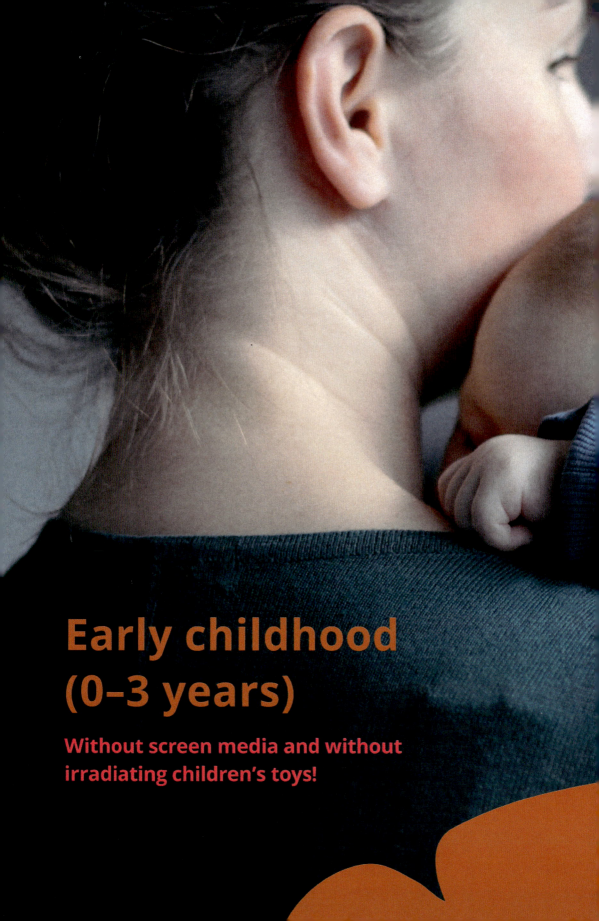

Early childhood (0–3 years)

Without screen media and without irradiating children's toys!

CHAPTER 3 EARLY CHILDHOOD (0–3 YEARS)

3.1 What do young children need for their healthy development?

For their entire further life it is decisive that children learn to be creative and imaginative. For this reason the actual environment of the child should contain various stimuli which challenge the imagination, as logical abstract thinking in adolescence develops from this.

Anything which takes away from the child the inner exertion of building his or her personal imaginative pictures should be excluded from the child's environment. This especially includes films and screen games which do not challenge the child's own creative ability.

For healthy development children need an environment which stimulates them in various ways. First and foremost it should encourage movement and should provoke the dexterity of grasping movements. A healthy environment for children is above all a space to move, a space which helps them to develop their fine and gross motor skills as much as possible.

To develop their senses in a healthy manner, children require direct experiences in the real world. It is thus very helpful if one can go out into nature as often as possible with young children, so that they can intensively experience animals and plants with the changes in the seasons and can include this in their play activities.

Children need consistent caregivers in their proximity who speak with them often. People with whom they can have conversations, people who tell them fairy tales, sagas and stories. It is of the utmost importance that people are talking to the child. Recordings with stories at this age are not meaningful.

For the nurturing of the parent-child bond it is very helpful to set aside a fixed time during the day in which the father or the mother does something together with the child. The length of time is less important than the intensity, the quality of the time spent together. Good bonding is a secure basis from which the child can actively explore the environment.

Tina (30) and Bernd (32) say:

When our little one (6 months) is awake, it is screen-free time. No PC, no smartphone and we hang a cloth over the television. A good side-effect of this is that the two bigger ones (5 and 8 years) also watch less than before, so as they say: Out of sight, out of mind. They have become great at entertaining themselves and do not need continual entertainment from the screen babysitter.[30]

If parents keep in mind the essential developmental steps of their children while they are growing up, they can more easily recognize and understand why and which limits are necessary in the use of digital media. Fundamental is "sensomotor integration," as described in this chapter. It forms a solid and necessary basis for later media maturity. The further stages 2 to 6 toward media maturity (see illustration below) are developed in the following age groups. Every stage has its very own justification and cannot be skipped. Otherwise the development of your child is significantly compromised and can be damaged.

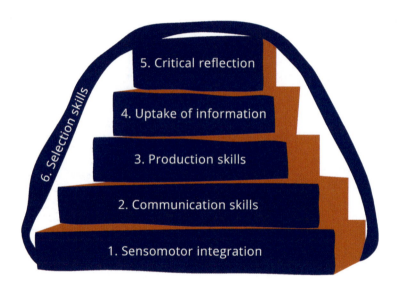

Developmental stages of the child before reaching media maturity
(see Bleckmann 2012[9] and suggested reading page 78)

3.2 Screen media has a different effect on children

There is a growing demand for "iToys," conventional toys with an integrated tablet or dolls and soft toys with built in Smart or baby phones, even for the youngest children.

iToys are intended to condition young children to the world of tomorrow.
This development, where we increasingly offer digital screen media to the youngest children, is cleverly associated with the message that it is important to introduce digital media as early as possible – already at early nursery school age – to children and adolescents, so that they can get used to digital media and prepare for the digital world.

This message is increasingly accepted (see miniKim-study 2014[10]) by many parents (in Germany by around 35%): the time that children spend in front of the screen of a tablet or smartphone is correspondingly increasing at a rapid rate (in the USA children younger than two years see screens already for 90 minutes per day). What does this mean for your child?

Why screen media is damaging to toddlers

For adults media presents a gateway into the world. For children it is different: The younger the child is, the greater the possible damage. The longer a child spends in front of a screen, the stronger the impairments in development can be. Why is this so?

For the maturity and growth of the brain a variety of sensory impressions are required: seeing, hearing, tasting, smelling, touching and feeling, a sense of gravity, the sense of one's own movement and many more. A newborn child needs six to eight years to substantially develop its senses.

The early use of interactive screen media provides a two-dimensional and therefore restricted sensory impression on a smooth, always consistent surface. The operation of this is mostly accompanied by a lack of movement experience within the entire body.

This one-sided, undemanding sensory experience mostly represents time lost for childhood development, as the joy in movement is missing. Healthy brain development is hindered as a result (Gertraud Teuchert-Noodt 2017, see suggested reading on page 17).

Watching television programs is damaging to a baby or toddler: The incomprehensible, often loud and garish content is overwhelming and can lead to anxiety and difficulty in sleeping. If the television is "merely" playing in the background, then speaking interaction and eye contact are both reduced. The delicate communicative signals of the adult are no longer perceived, as has been shown by the recent research results of speech researchers.

Screen media takes the place of direct contact with the real world and with other people. Pediatricians thus recommend: Do not expose your child to a screen! Also not passively. Children learn to speak better by the end of nursery school the more they have a media-free environment – alone and also together with their parents.

Television, tablet and smartphone time is non-talking time
Telephoning or chatting parents are physically present, but are only "incidentally" involved with their child. The same is true for parents using a tablet or PC. Bonding researchers warn:

An excessive use of TV, PC/tablet and smartphone disturbs the parent-child bond. This can be damaging to the relationship!

For the secure bonding between the parents and child, the first months and years of life are especially important. A stable parent-child relationship, where direct contact with the child is not shared by media, is an indispensible foundation for your child's healthy and happy life – and a bonus for the parents.

Suggested reading

Susan Greenfield (2014)
Mind Change – How Digital Technologies Are Leaving Their Mark on Our Brains, Random House

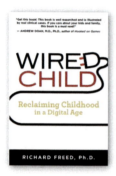

Richard Freed (2015)
Wired Child; Reclaiming Childhood in a Digital Age, Create Space Independent Publishing Platform

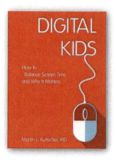

Martin L Kutscher, MD (2016)
Digital Kids, Jessica Kingsley Publishers

Internet:

Delaney Ruston MD (2018)
Groundbreaking Study Discovers an Association between Screen Time and Actual Brain Changes, Tech-Talk-Tuesday blog on 'Screenagers: Growing up in the Digital Age,' www.screenagersmovie.com/tech-talk-tuesdays/groundbreaking-study-discovers-an-association-between-screen-time-and-actual-brain-changes

Experiences Build Brain Architecture, Harvard University Center on the Developing Child, YouTube video, youtu.be/VNNsN9IJkws

3.3 Responsible media education during early childhood

- *The times of intensive affection toward your child with a lot of physical contact and closeness are very important for the mother and child. Allow yourself these free times!*

- *Quiet times are important for your baby* because then he or she has the leisure to explore his or her own body and environment.

- *You also need time to rest.* Therefore get your child used to entertaining him- or herself a bit. Even a young child can do that. First for five, then ten, then fifteen minutes. It may be an effort in the beginning, but over the years it is an advantage for the parents and for the child.

- *The environment for early childhood should ideally be free of technical media.* There should be no television, computer or smartphone in the immediate environment of the child.

- *Your child does not need screen-based toys.* The featureless surface and the one-sided operations (swiping and tapping) only inadequately stimulate the development of the brain. The mobile wireless radiation which is often connected to such toys is a danger to the biological development of your child which should be taken seriously!

- *Recommended "media" for early childhood*: human language, directed at your child, books which are read or looked at together, and music which is made by oneself or listened to together.

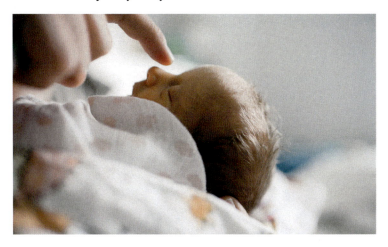

Nursery school age (4–6 years)

Real world experience and movement – as much as possible!

CHAPTER 4 NURSERY SCHOOL AGE (4–6 YEARS)

4.1 What do children need for their healthy development?

It is important that children, through many varied primary experiences, encounter the real, analogue world in as many aspects as possible. All of this together promotes the healthy growth of the brain and creates the basis in later years for successful learning.

- For the *development of the senses and sensomotor integration* children need a variety of unmediated experiences: natural phenomena, experiences in the country and with animals, with instruments, etc.
- For the *development of fine motor skills and creativity* frequent encouragement to draw, craft, sculpt, etc., are very helpful. The repeated experience of children that they can make something themselves contributes to their self-confidence.
- *Cognitive development* is promoted by lots of movement.
- Real instead of virtual play *promotes creativity*. The possibility of exploring "mysterious" (but safe) play environments, and to do this with others of the same age, should be offered repeatedly.
- A *manageable spatial environment* and a *rhythmic repetition of daily events* provide a sense of security.
- Direct contact with other people stimulates the *development of speech*.
- *Interest and attention* from the parents strengthen the parent-child bond: "You are important to us!"
- *A lot of physical contact* with others, especially within the family, stimulates all the senses.

Suggested reading

Richard House, editor (2011)
Too Much, Too Soon, Hawthorn Press

Wendy Ellyatt (2017)
Healthy and Happy – Children's Wellbeing in the 2020s, Save Childhood Movement. Available as a PDF document: www.savechildhood.net/wp-content/uploads/2017/11/Healthy-and-Happy-W-Ellyatt-Full-paper-2017-v2.pdf

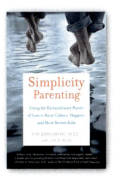

Kim John Payne (2010)
Simplicity Parenting: Using the Extraordinary Power of Less to Raise Calmer, Happier and More Secure Kids, Ballantine Books

4.2 This is the effect of screen media at nursery school age

All screen media, such as TV, PC, smartphone, Gameboy, etc., activate only eyes and ears. The other senses are hardly stimulated at all. This disables the development of fine motor skills, but, above all, sensomotor integration (the connection of sensory experiences).

Extensive or frequent consumption of screen media replaces the time the child can spend with other people and shortens the time for direct contact with the real world.

Screen media reduces speech communication with other people, and the child's imagination withers as a result of alien images. Initially a restless child is captured in front of the screen, but afterward the restlessness increases.

Time in front of the screen reduces the movement radius of the child and promotes lack of motion. As a result, excessive weight, postural damage, short-sightedness, among others, are common. "According to the latest BLIKK study, 70% of the children in nursery school use their parent's smartphone for more than a half hour. The results are disturbances in speech development and concentration, physical hyperactivity, inner restlessness, through to aggressive behavior."[1][11]

Therefore: Limit the time children spend in front of a screen. This applies to TV and computers of any kind, as well as tablets, smartphones, Gameboys, etc.

4.3 Responsible media education at nursery school age

The appropriate, competent and creative handling of the possibilities of screen media does not presuppose technical and mental abilities which have to be learned in childhood. For this reason the development of speech ability and creativity are prioritized during nursery school age. Therefore, storytelling, children's books and – in moderation – audio media are suggested. Regular time reading to your child and also bedtime stories which are told freestyle are mutually enjoyable and give the child a sense of security. In addition, this is preparation for later reading readiness.

- No screen devices (TV, PC, tablet, etc.) in the child's room!

- Television/films should be restricted to 10 to 20 minutes per day – but not every day – and once a week for half an hour.

- If your child wants to watch a children's film, then watch the film with your child. In this way the entertainment is a communal experience and your child can share his or her questions and experiences directly with you.

- Beware of advertisements! Better than commercial television are DVDs (no advertisements, short programs). This way you avoid much of the grueling, whining ("Mommy, buy that for me!").

- Get the grandparents "on board." The rules set by the parents can be applied without (or at least with less) stress. Agreements with the parents of your children's friends can also be very helpful.

Nadja (35) single parent, Lukas (10) and Johanna (5):

With Lukas I used withholding TV as a threat: "If you don't tidy up, then no TV!" That really degenerated. Eventually he wouldn't do anything without being threatened by "TV withdrawal." It was stressful rather than a solution. It was difficult to get out of that situation again, but we managed. With the little one from the beginning I didn't allow myself to get sucked in.[30]

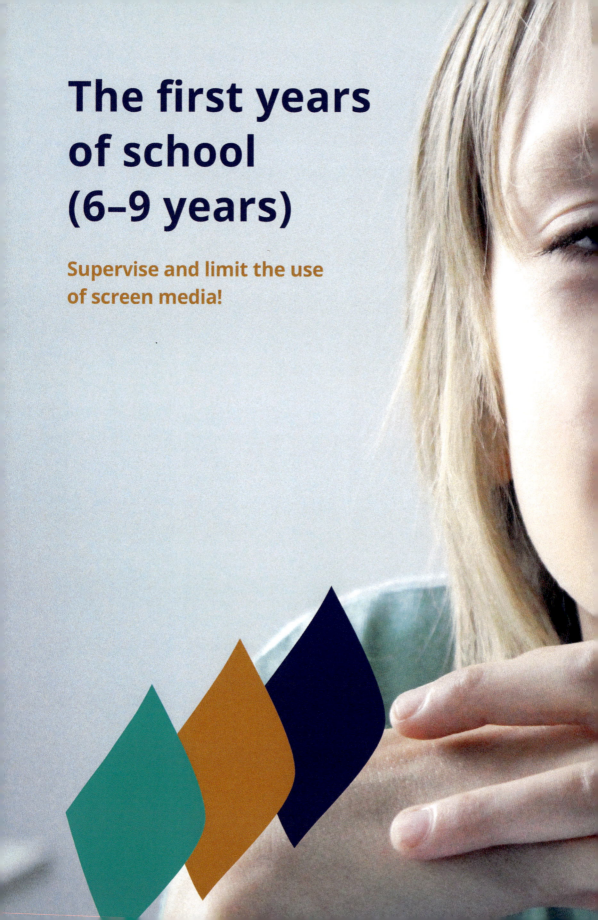

The first years of school (6–9 years)

Supervise and limit the use of screen media!

CHAPTER 5 THE FIRST YEARS OF SCHOOL (6–9 YEARS)

5.1 Developmental steps in the primary school years

Mastering reading and writing is a prerequisite for the use of modern media. By specializing children too early in the use of computers for acquiring knowledge, due to a presumed requirement of modernity, one ultimately makes them media incompetent. Computers have not replaced books, but have been added as an enhancement.

The emphasis in child development is on the acquisition of *cultural abilities*: Now they can ride a bicycle, go on a skateboard, learn to swim, understand how to use tools meaningfully, learn to master an instrument and above all, *write, read and calculate*. Children thus profit much more if they are supported in learning how to read – rather than in the consumption of media – so they can, *together with father or mother*, conquer the universe of children's literature.

The circle of childhood relationships expands beyond the family. Especially *friendships with children of the same age* become very important. Here conflicts often develop. The children here have to learn to understand others, to consider them, etc.

In such situations it is very important that the adults are perceived as trustworthy and can thus be examples of how to deal with anger, rage or aggression.

The child is not yet able to precisely evaluate his abilities. One should thus protect him or her from big mistakes. However, *over-protection damages self-confidence*. Mistakes and failures are a necessary part of life and of learning. Those who continue despite obstacles and are *successful*, gain in *self-assurance* and learn to correctly evaluate themselves.

5.2 Psychologists and pediatricians describe the fundamental needs of children

The following fundamental needs of children, the fulfillment of which considerably contribute to their healthy development, were formulated by pediatricians based on their own observations. The most important are:[31]

- *Reliable love and security*
  Children desire a stable, reliable and loving relationship with their parents and their social environment. Included in this is the reliability and manageability of everyday occurrences.

- *Praise and recognition*
  Especially in the school environment children need a positive prevailing mood which strengthens their self-confidence.

- *New developmentally appropriate experiences*
  Children are curious. They want to discover the world, absorb new experiences, thoughts, images, feelings, and above all gain new motor skills. While growing up, children have to master a series of developmental steps, for the attainment of which they need very particular experiences.

Examples:

Independence and responsibility
In every child there is an independent individuality who wants to develop. This requires training fields in which the first steps toward acquiring independent responsibility can be tried and practised.

Boundaries and structure
For the development of a healthy experience of identity children need clear, meaningful rules and boundaries, which the children respect as a result of the bonding experiences with their caregivers.

- Physical integrity and security
  It is a general and self-evident conviction that this fundamental need of children is respected. Again and again we see that this fundamental need is disregarded worldwide.

5.3 Responsible media education at primary school age

Encourage your child to develop friendships, to play sports, to learn an instrument! Surprising but true: This is the best prevention against computer game addiction, cyberbullying, contents which are inappropriate for children and swindles on the internet. Such a solid anchoring in life, real success and true recognition, protect the child from seeking "cheap" substitutes in virtual life.

- *No screen devices in the child's room.* Children with their own TV spend about one hour more in front of a screen than children without their own TV.

- *Clear time limits*: 30 to max 45 minutes per day, but above all, children should not spend time in front of a screen (television, tablet, PC) every day, weekly at most five hours (see section 6.5). With more than five hours weekly in front of a screen their reading and calculation abilities become impaired.

- *If at all possible, no PC or internet usage.* If this is not possible, then ensure that your child uses the PC or internet accompanied by an adult. Speak to your children about the contents and what he or she experiences. In this way you can nurture the media maturity of your children.

- If it is not always possible to accompany your children while they are using the PC, then *create their own user account* for your children on the PC, laptop or tablet with limited rights (in the control panel or user accounts).

- Activate time limits with *time limiting software* (per day and per week) and install *child safety software* (see section 6.5).

- Children between six and nine years should – if at all – only be allowed in *safe surf domains* and not on sites like YouTube: YouTube's portal also contains films and advertisements which are unsuitable for children.

- A safe domain to surf from which has been created especially for children so that they can move within the internet without encountering content which is unsuitable. There are a number of possibilities – each site or app will have its strengths and weaknesses, depending on what you are looking for. For a listing of kid-safe browsers and search sites, see www.commonsensemedia.org and search for "kid safe browsers"; alternately see under "Parenting Apps" at www.screenagersmovie.com/parenting-apps. Some operate on a single device, others over multiple devices for the whole family including mobile phones. Choose those that do not require Wi-Fi for setting up, and ensure that the devices are connected to the internet by means of a cable and not over Wi-Fi (see page 41).

- Some special search engines for children are given on www.safesearchkids.com. Install a children's search engine as a browser start page! A search engine for children often needs coupling with a safe browser (see last bullet point) as some bring up links which take you outside of a kids' domain within another click or two.

- Protect access to app-stores with a password so that your children cannot download apps themselves. Be wary of free offers! Always download apps yourself and try them out before your child plays with them alone. Check whether the agreement which the app requires spies on your private sphere – if it does, then do not install under any circumstances! Always deactivate automatic updates so that you can check whether there are new costs or agreements.

- App recommendations for children – arranged according to age – can be found under: www.commonsensemedia.org/app-reviews. There are also other sites – search for "app recommendations for kids." Note that on many sites the age recommendations are from the app developers and not necessarily neutral bodies. Parents will need to exercise their own discretion.

- Observe the voluntary age restrictions set by the film industry (Film Rating System of the Motion Picture Association of America: www.mpaa.org or British Board of Film Classification: www.bbfc.co.uk) and entertainment software ratings (Entertainment Software Rating Board: www.esrb.org) (see pages 73 and 123).

- In the lower grades PC homework should remain a rare exception. If it is unavoidable, then demand a supervised media room at the school. Then: no PC and internet usage without protective software or adult supervision.

- No personal mobile or smartphone for your child at primary school age! If it has to be, then restricted to telephone and SMS usage (see section 6.5)! Internet access (e.g., at a flat rate) is not recommended as it carries many risks.

Tobias (38) and Maria (32) say:

When Jonas had problems with learning to read, everyone recommended: Read to him more, less television, less time on the games console and with DVDs. Jonas now is allowed screen access only on weekends. The expected big protest did not happen. Admittedly, the first few weeks were really hard, there was a lot of boredom and whining. But now, because of the clear rules, it is a lot more relaxed. And Jonas' reading has improved a lot.[30]

- New Zealand, Dr. Arie Sigman: Report to Family First, NZ 2015: "Media Use An Emerging Factor in Child and Adolescent Health
- World Health Organization (WHO) 24 April 2019, Digital Media Guidelines.

From childhood to adolescence (10–16 years)

On the path to media maturity

CHAPTER 6   FROM CHILDHOOD TO ADOLESCENCE (10–16 YEARS)

6.1 What do adolescents need for their healthy development?

Puberty is a time of massive physical and emotional changes. Mood swings are often a part of everyday life. The child emerges from the sense of social protection which he or she has had until now and seeks his or her own rootedness in the world. This is a long process which occurs over many years. During this time, adolescents have to master a series of developmental steps.

Forming and building up an identity

Perhaps the most important task is the formation and the building up of one's own identity. This includes a positive relationship with the changes within one's own body, but also the newly emerging irritating feelings. Above all, adolescents have to satisfactorily answer the question, "Who am I?" Just as the toddler had to learn to walk upright, the adolescent has to find his or her own inner standpoint and learn to assert it in life.

Building up social relationships

A further great developmental step for adolescents comes in building up social relationships and meeting the requirements of the accompanying responsibilities. Friendships within the same age group continue to gain in importance.

What meaning do I want to give my life?

A third developmental task for adolescents lies in the practical question about what they want to achieve in life, which education they want to attain and, furthermore, how life goals can be realized. "What is my life goal and what do I have to do so that I can realize it?" – this is the fundamental question of adolescence, which is often carried over into young adulthood.

Adolescents often come across as a lot older than they actually are! Premature sexualization is especially enhanced by the world of media and advertising. It is thus all the more important to create counterbalances. Not an easy task for parents: Allowing a healthy measure of independence but also maintaining the responsibility for it.

6.2 The impact of screen media

Between the ages of 10 and 16 years the relationship of children to media changes. They are fascinated by the digital world, smartphone, computer and internet, all of which become increasingly important to them:
- At the age of 12, around three out of four children are on the internet alone.
- They engage increasingly on social media networks (Facebook, Instagram) and intensively use digital communication (WhatsApp among others).
- Above all they look for entertainment on the internet (games, movies, music).

However:
Children and soon-to-be adolescents do not yet possess the mature discretion and life experience of adults. They are not yet able to recognize and see through clever marketing methods or ideologically influenced texts.

The perception that children as "digital natives" are more capable of finding their way on the internet than adults is not true: This misjudges the important fact that, with all their skill in operating the systems, children lack the ability to appropriately understand the pros and cons of what the internet offers. The age ratings (MPAA or BBFC and ESRB, see pages 68 and 123) are still important, but are in many cases ignored. Adolescents have to learn to protect themselves against the addictive potential of what media offers. Giving them their own devices thus only creates problems! (see chapter 7)

The internet portal www.safekids.co.uk summarizes the dangers facing children and adolescents with the formula "CCCC" (Content, Commerce, Contact, Culture):
- Content not suitable for children: pornography, anorexia forums, representations of violence, tasteless videos, right and left radicalism, Satanism, etc.
- Commercial seduction: advertisements, aggressive marketing, spam, poker pages, erotic offers, etc.
- Contact: false contacts, verbal sexual abuse by pedophiles, real abuse as a result of physical contact, etc.
- Culture: bullying, downloading of illegal music data, games, films, copyright contraventions, etc.

For the ages between 10 and 13 years, the authors thus recommend:
- No account on Facebook, WhatsApp or other information services: According to EU General Data Protection Regulation, an account without parental consent is only legal from the age of 16 years (see www.eugdpr.org, art. 8). If the child is younger than 16 years, the parents have to give consent for an account. They then have a legal obligation to supervise and monitor its use (see section 8.5).
- No mobile devices (smartphone, tablet, etc.).
- No screen devices in the child's room.

Suggested reading

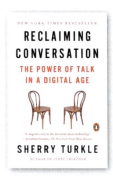

Sherry Turkle (2016)
Reclaiming Conversation: The Power of Talk in a Digital Age, Penguin Press

Janell Burley Hofmann (2014)
iRules: What Every Tech-Healthy Family Needs to Know about Selfies, Sexting, Gaming and Growing Up, Rodale Books

Children's Well-being in UK, Sweden and Spain: The Role of Inequality and Materialism, Ipsos MORI Social Research Institute in Partnership with Dr. Agnes Nairn (2011). Available as a PDF document: agnesnairn.co.uk/policy_reports/child-well-being-report.pdf

6.3 Growing into mature and healthy media usage

Children/adolescents (10 to 16 years of age) need a healthy measure of freedom for independent action, but also clear rules. Do not enforce strict bans, instead invest time in explanations, and do not spy on your children. Support (non-media) interests, thereby providing a counterbalance to media consumption.

- For parents with adolescents: a communal internet PC, e.g., in the living room or kitchen area. There may be more negotiations about who is allowed to use it when, but parents can in this way supervise time and content.

- If your child is using an internet PC without supervision, then absolutely install time-limiting and filter software, such as Net Nanny (See sections 1.3 and 6.5).

- Also install feature and time limiting apps on the smartphone (see www.screenagersmovie.com/parenting-apps and sections 1.3 and 6.5, page 84).

- As soon as there is access to internet on a personal PC or smartphone (not earlier than 12 years, however it is better if it is later – as late as possible), then agree in writing on time limits (e.g., seven hours per week) in the framework of a media use contract. (Suggestions about this can be found at www.screenagersmovie.com/contracts or with the search keywords "media usage contract.")

- Furthermore, you need to think about and negotiate consequences for when the rules or the contract are not upheld! It has to be clear to your children which sanction you will implement in the case of offenses. Implement your measures consistently. It is worth it to quietly bear conflicts so that, more importantly, stress, radiation and the risk of addiction are avoided.

- Fundamentally the recommendation holds: Mobile devices (smartphone, tablet) and the internet should be used only within time limits and be run implementing radiation minimization (see section 2.2).

- Using limited, well chosen educational films and educational software your children can be supported in their learning process (see section 6.4).

- Educate about dangers and legal regulations. Often, in dealing with their own images or sound recordings, or those of others, children do not have any sense of culpability (see chapter 8).

- Explain what children/adolescents are not allowed to do. Whoever tolerates actions which fall in the sphere of culpability, is behaving extremely irresponsibly toward their children.

- Store smartphone outside children's bedrooms at night.

- Growing into media maturity – independent media usage requires time.

Media maturity involves recognizing and evaluating the chances and risks associated with the new media – especially the seduction of long-term use, the dangers of addiction, the surveillance, the loss of privacy and the accompanying dangers of manipulation, as well as radiation risks, among others – and deciding about the kind and quantity of media usage. Media maturity can thus also mean that adolescents choose non-media alternatives, which protect them from many risks, e.g., a landline instead of a smartphone.

Suggested reading

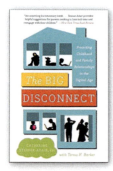

Catherine Steiner-Adair (2014)
The Big Disconnect: Protecting Childhood and Family Relationships in the Digital Age, Harper Paperbacks

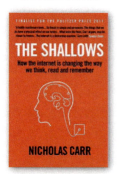

Nicholas Carr (2010)
The Shallows – How the Internet Is Changing the Way We Think, Read and Remember, Atlantic books

Wendy Ellyatt (2018)
Technology and the Future of Childhood, Save Childhood Movement. Available as a PDF document:
www.savechildhood.net/wp-content/uploads/2017/11/DIGITAL-CHILDHOOD-Save-Childhood-Movement-1.pdf

Internet:

Delaney Ruston MD (2019)
Screen-Free Zones – How to Encourage More Face to Face Time, Tech-Talk-Tuesday blog on 'Screenagers: Growing up in the Digital Age,'
www.screenagersmovie.com/tech-talk-tuesdays/screen-free-zones-how-to-encourage-more-face-to-face-time

6.4 Long-term learning with new media

A personal PC in the child's bedroom?

The more screen media devices there are in the child's own room, the more time adolescents spend using these devices. Unsuitable films and computer games (age 16/18) are used far more frequently if the child owns a personal device. Therefore: No screen media in the child's room!

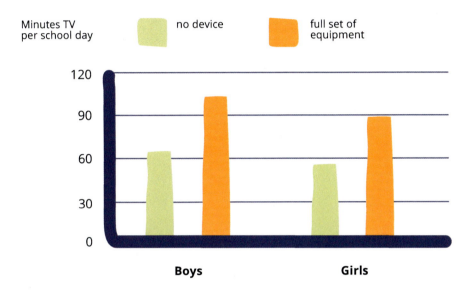

This is easier said than done. Who is not familiar with: "Mommy, Daddy, but all the other kids have it!" What can help parents to serenely and reasonably say no? The certainty that long-term you are doing your child a favor. You are protecting him or her from the dangers of screen media: violence, pornography, bullying, addiction. And the child has more time for what he or she actually wants: to play outside and to meet with friends. According to a survey these are the favorite free time activities of German primary school children.

And if older children need to work on a PC and internet for school? Then they do not need a personal device for this. They can use a communal "parent PC" for this purpose, which is then turned off afterward.

Are PCs, TVs, and mobile phones useful for learning?
On the one hand:
Research has shown that, in the case of older children and adults, the controlled use of digital media is useful as a supportive tool for learning.
Examples: a PC language course for refreshing Spanish language skills, a training program for dyslexics, a film about deep sea fishes. However, a "hard-copy encyclopedia" is recommended for a geography paper about Thailand. Why? Because on Google and other such search engines such a search very quickly takes one to the page of a sex hotel.

On the other hand:
The more time children spend in front of screen media, the poorer their school performance is. Scientists particularly explain this negative correlation in this way: For successful and independent problem solving and learning, children need experiences in real life. TV, PCs, and mobile phones are considered to be time thieves and replace learning involving all the senses. Additionally, motivation suffers: a school book seems somehow boring and tedious if one is very used to bright, loud, fast video clips.

Conclusion:
For long-term learning children need support without performance pressure from their parents, a good social environment in class, and teachers who are convincing in terms of subject and as people.

It is also important to guard against too much screen media. The younger the child is, the longer the usage times and the more violent the content, the more damage the screen media inflicts. The better the age appropriate introduction succeeds, the more TV, PCs, and mobile phones can contribute to thinking, researching and learning.

Suggested reading

Joe Clement and Matt Miles (2018)
Screen Schooled – Two Veteran Teachers Expose How Technology Overuse Is Making Our Kids Dumber, Black Inc.

Aric Sigman (2015)
Practically Minded: The Benefits and Mechanisms Associated with a Practical Skills-based Curriculum. Available as a PDF document: www.rmt.org/wp-content/uploads/2018/09/Practically-Minded-2015.pdf

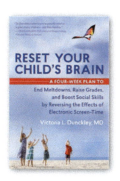

Victoria Dunkley, MD (2015)
Reset Your Child's Brain: A Four-week Plan to End Meltdowns, Raise Grades and Boost Social Skills by Reversing the Effects of Electronic Screen-time, New World Library

6.5 Security software and technical support

In general we can say:
- Technology can in a limited way contribute to protecting young children from youth-endangering content, swindles and undesirable contacts on the internet.
- Some protective mechanisms are available as standard on smartphones and other devices and only have to be activated. Others are easy to download and install as software/apps.
- Technical safety alone is not enough. Parents have to talk to their children about the appropriate way to behave online, to minimize the risks (see chapters 7 and 8).

In particular this means: On your home PC, laptop or tablet, set up user content for your children with limited rights. Activate time-limiting software (per day and for the whole week) and install child safety software – also called filter software.

Listed below are some examples of time limiting and child safety software which are currently available on the market. Whether this software really is good cannot be guaranteed. For a comprehensive listing and review of 'Screen Time Management Apps' see: www.screenagersmovie.com/parenting-apps. Additional child safety software, as well as tests of the different options, can also be found under the keyword search "child safety software" in all search engines.

The Screenagers website also provides useful information on all aspects of working with your children and teenagers to help them find a healthy relationship to mobile phone and screen usage. The feature length movie, entitled Screenagers, has been influential in shaping policies in the USA. See www.screenagersmovie.com.

For PC and Mac (some of these cover mobile phones as well):
- Salfeld parental control (free download): salfeld.com/en
- Kaspersky Total Security: www.kaspersky.co.uk/total-security
- Net Nanny: www.netnanny.com. A popular application, but one review says more effective on computers than mobile phones.
- Microsoft Family Safety (built in to Windows 8 and later operating sytems, free): Go to the control panel for setting up a child's account. From here you can choose filters and time controls.
- On Mac OS, go to Parental Controls under "Preferences" (free).

Your internet browser will also have whitelist and blacklist functions (free).

Some routers have built in parental control options. If not you can set up an OpenDNS account (search for "OpenDNS router parental controls" for instructions – it is safe, and reversible). Note that this may apply the same filters and controls to all users on the network, though some can apply separate filters to different IP addresses on the network. This is also a free option.

As soon as unsupervised internet usage with a personal tablet or smartphone is possible, install functional and time limiting software or apps.

Additional examples for mobile phones. Most can be used with both Android and Apple mobiles:
- **SPACE, formerly called Breakfree App:** findyourphonelifebalance.com
- **FamilyTime,** familytime.io
- **Our Pact,** ourpact.com
- **Moment,** inthemoment.io, for Android and Apple. More for older children and adults, this has a 'coaching' function to help get you off the phone more.
- Screen Time and App Limits features as part of Apple's new iOS12 phones

See www.screenagersmovie.com/parenting-apps for descriptions of each of the above.

CHAPTER 6 FROM CHILDHOOD TO ADOLESCENCE (10–16 YERARS)

CHAPTER 7   THE DANGERS OF USING DIGITAL MEDIA

7.1 Stress associated with social media

The JIM study[12] which appeared in Spring of 2017, shows that the use of digital mobile devices and the corresponding communication apps by adolescents between the ages of 12 and 19 is increasing. The application WhatsApp is used by 95% of adolescents, followed by Instagram (51%) and Snapchat (45%), as well as Facebook (43%). These electronic aids are firmly anchored in the everyday communications of young people. The time spent on use daily is typically 2.5 hours for 12- to 13-year-olds, well over 3 hours for 14- to 15-year-olds, and almost 4 hours for 16- to 19-year-olds.

The communication freedom – to be reachable constantly and everywhere – is a blessing and a curse at the same time. Adolescents are increasingly complaining about communication stress, caused among other things by up to 3,000 WhatsApp messages per month which are read and written.[13] Also, according to a 2015 study commissioned by the State Media Authority in North Rhine-Westphalia, 120 of 500 questioned children and adolescents between the ages of 8 and 14 years (i.e., 24%) feel stressed as a result of the permanent communication over messenger services such as WhatsApp.[1 11] 240 out of 500 (i.e., 48%) admit to being distracted by a mobile phone, for example, from homework.

Ever more adolescents are subjected to continual communication from first thing in the morning through late into the night, to the unspoken and unquestioned demand to react immediately whenever it prompts – and this begins straight after getting up and carries on until late in the night. The social pressure of the peer group with its seemingly inescapable obligation to be constantly available and constantly reactive means a very high level of stress. Conversely, not being in constant communication evokes a feeling of social isolation and loneliness in these adolescents: this new stress condition is called Fomo, Fear of Missing Out.

According to a study by the smartphone manufacturer Nokia, young people use their smartphone up to 150 times a day. If 100 messages have to be read and answered daily, the practically constant usage of communication media cannot remain without effect: it compulsively leads to frequent interruptions of other activities (on average about every 9–10 minutes) and thus leads to constant multi-tasking[13].

The influence on cognition and learning

Multi-tasking – when all manner of things are continually done concurrently – requires a continual switching of attention, which can lead to so-called attentiveness stress: For example, the student who works at the computer is actually busy with other things besides homework for almost two thirds of the time.

The spans of time in which adolescents are devoted to only one thing is constantly decreasing due to multi-tasking. Recently Microsoft published a study which shows that the *attention span* of 12 seconds in the year 2000 *has decreased to eight seconds in the year 2013*. The attention span of goldfish, at nine seconds, is thus even a second higher. A decreasing attention span means a decreasing ability to concentrate.[13]

Multi-taskers are effectively on the way to attention disorder[14][15]: They find it very difficult not to follow up on irrelevant tasks and to ignore irritants from their environment or in their minds. The effect is superficiality and ineffectuality in handling important tasks and, above all, in learning, as the brain grows tired and its uptake ability is exhausted due to the density of stimuli. What has been newly learned is thus only anchored in long-term memory in a limited way: Because the brain needs times of rest to reflect on and consolidate what has been learned, which multi-tasking does not allow.

- Speech competency deteriorates, as well as tactile capabilities. Because the featureless surface of a smartphone leaves behind a uniform, structureless tactile impression in our brain. "When we touch and move something in the real world, this influences our cognitive conceptual ability more than we had realized before." (Martin Korte 2010[16])
- Reading is also increasingly on the decline. The proportion of non-readers among children, those who never take a book into their hands, has almost quadrupled: In 2005 it was 7%, in 2014 already 25%. The highest proportion of non-readers at 35%, is among 16- to 17-year-olds, particularly those adolescents with a low level of formal education.[12]

Mental disorders

Besides the effect on concentration and memory, communication stress manifests, above all, in restlessness, nervousness, irritability and headaches, which have all increased dramatically over the last few years. Sleep disturbances and tiredness during the day are also continually increasing. These could also be a result of communication on a smartphone well into the night. Other mental disorders cannot be precluded (heart complaints, irrational fears right up to depression, among others), which are elicited or enhanced by steady wireless communications radiation (see chapter 2).

Influence on social life

In a 2014 study by BITKOM, over 1,000 adolescents were asked in which situations smartphones, Facebook, etc., are irritating. The answers show that adolescents are capable of accurately reflecting on the influences mobile phones have on their lives. A boy wrote: "It bothers me most when I am tired and would like to go to sleep. Because of it I get too little sleep." And a girl said: "Actually in every situation, because one is looking at it all the time and so much time is lost." The most frequent criticism is that friendships are endangered by smartphones. One participant explained: "My friends spend more time on their phones than with me. At the moment they place virtual life above reality, even though only real life creates the experiences and feelings which we will remember later."[18]

Beatrice does not like the fact that when she goes out with her friends, they only play on their mobile devices: "Somehow everyone is distracted and it is irritating when I have to say everything three times because no one really listens anymore. Only my grandparents are still able to listen." They, coincidentally, do not have a mobile phone.

The unthinking tendency to be permanently online and at all times ready to react, has fundamentally impacted the lives of adolescents and their interactions, exchanges and bonding with others. The mobile phone has become more important than the person with you. The digital world is replacing direct social contact. Despite all this communication, there is social isolation. The (side-) effects of this "flight" into the world of virtual communication can already be clearly observed:

- The ability of adolescents to appropriately interpret social signals is stunted. This can be seen in the lack or complete absence of social-empathetic behavior and constructive, socially acceptable conflict behavior within peer groups. A study[19] by US psychologist Sarah Konrath shows that the ability of college students to be empathetic had decreased since 1990 by about 40%. Narcissistic-egotistical communication behavior predominates in combination with an increased tendency to self-representation (among others by means of selfies and the likes).
- The non-binding nature is also increasing: Whereas previously arrangements to meet were made and as a rule carried out, today personal time planning is constantly subjected to new negotiations, arrangements and changes of plan. Arrangements often only take place with provisos.

- Adolescents rarely have a chance to choose how to fill their free time. Meeting with others, sports and reading are neglected, as it is much easier to fall back on an easily accessible and short-term medium such as a smartphone, iPod or Xbox. As a result individuality and creativity are deteriorating.

What is important?
If adolescents spend a lot of time on the internet, it need not in itself be a cause for concern, as long as direct social contacts and hobbies are still nurtured and school work does not suffer. The effect of the use of digital communication and entertainment should, however, not be underestimated (see section 7.2).

Adolescents are increasingly sensing the disproportionate nature of the situation: They would not like to manage without digital communication, but are irritated by the high level of messages they receive and reject the dictatorship of having to answer immediately. They do not want to be slaves to the fast pace. The perception that it must be urgent whenever the mobile rings, is a compulsion, a dilemma, from which young people often cannot escape on their own. Adolescents must, among other things, learn to reduce discussions to the most essential points. They have to learn to consciously decide what they allow into their heads.

What can you as a parent do? Start the discussion with your children and try to bring about a balance between media and other free time activities. If nothing else, technical means – such as time limiting software – can help to find an appropriate balance (see section 6.5). If necessary, seek out professional help (see section 7.2).

Suggested reading

Jean M. Twenge (2018)
iGen: Why Today's Super-Connected Kids Are Growing Up Less Rebellious, More Tolerant, Less Happy – and Completely Unprepared for Adulthood – and What That Means for the Rest of Us, Atria Books

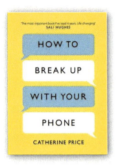

Catherine Price (2018)
How to Break up with Your Phone: The 30-Day Plan to Take Back Your Life, Trapeze

Tanya Goodin (2017)
OFF. Your Digital Detox for a Better Life, Ilex Press

7.2 Excessive media use and the dangers of addiction

*"I fear the day that technology will
surpass our human interaction.
The world will have a generation of idiots."*

Albert Einstein

The DAK study of 2015 "Internetsucht im Kinderzimmer" ("Internet addiction in the children's room")[20] confirms a considerable worldwide development among adolescents, and even among children, with alarming figures: In 50% of 12- to 17-year-olds daily internet usage is already at two to three hours a day. On weekends the time spent reaches an average of four hours. On a Saturday or Sunday, 20% of the boys and girls spend six hours or more on computer games or internet usage.

The risks of media usage are ever clearer: 22% of children and adolescents feel restless, moody or irritable when they have to reduce their internet consumption. Already 5% (that is about 120,000) suffer from pathological consequences of internet usage, and around 8% already display an increased risk of internet addiction, i.e., they spend 8 to 10 hours per day on games and compulsively neglect their other activities.

Studies and surveys about internet addiction in 12- to 17-year-olds

50 %
surf on the internet for 2–3 hours daily, on weekends for up to 6 hours

 22 %
feel restless, moody or irritable when they have to reduce their internet consumption

60 %
of 9- and 10-year-olds can at most occupy themselves for half an hour without a television, computer or other digital media

 40 %
of 13-year-olds display learning and concentration disturbances

A survey of pediatric practices in North Rhine-Westphalia in 2015, within the context of the BLIKK Media Study[11] of the Drug Commission of the Federal Republic of Germany (Drogenbeauftragten der Bundesregierung), showed: "More than 60% of 9- to 10-year-olds in Germany can at most keep busy for half an hour without television, computer or other digital media. 40% of 13-year-olds additionally displayed learning and concentration disturbances." Many parents also complained that their children, preferring computer games and television, neglect other activities such as reading books.

Medical doctor and media therapist Bert te Wildt in his book, *Digital Junkies*,[34] describes smartphones as an unmistakable addictive medium and starter drug: "By intentionally built-in reward mechanisms the user is riveted to the device and his self-control is switched off."[24]

Children and adolescents are increasingly becoming addicted to the internet!
The parents of Max (16 years) came for a consultation.
Diana (35) says:

We were always so proud of Max and always wanted the best for him. As a reward for good marks we gave him new computer games. When he kicked in the door last week because I switched off the internet, we woke up. For months already Max has been living almost completely in his online world. His performance at school has dropped. Kurt and Paul also do not visit anymore. He gave up football ages ago. Max himself sees no problem, but we are desperate and do not know what to do.[30]

In the end Max was diagnosed with computer game addiction. For other worried parents the counselor could provide an all-clear or help them with a few suggestions.

Max is no exception! The addictive potential of digital media overwhelms us all, but especially children and adolescents. According to a 2016 DAK study, in the age group 12–15 years, 5.7% (about 696,000 people) are affected by computer game addiction, males at 8.4% clearly more dependent than females.[21] This is confirmed by a more recent study by the Federal Center of Health Education (Bundeszentrale für gesundheitliche Auflklärung or BZgA) in Germany of February 2017 ("The drug affinity of adolescents in the Federal Republic of Germany 2015, volume computer games and internet"). Approximately 270,000 adolescents between 12–17 years – which corresponds to a ratio of 5.8% – have a "computer game or internet related disturbance." The number almost doubled within 4 years since 2011 (from 3% to 5.3%). Whereas boys spend most their time on online games, girls mostly use the internet for communication. Among 12- to 13-year-olds, according to the DAK study "internet addiction in the child's room" already affects 3.9% (65,000 children).

It is thus not surprising that children and adolescents increasingly have to be treated: Looking just at cases at the German Center for Addiction in Children and Adolescents (Deutschen Zentrum für Suchtfragen des Kindes- und Jugendalters) at the University clinic of Hamburg-Eppendorf, there are 400 internet-addicted children and adolescents per year alone. About every tenth child uses the internet to escape from problems. Experts argue that in Germany up to one million people could be addicted to the internet.

Using 24 hours sensibly – beware of time thieves

Warning signs

The first signs of excessive internet usage often go unnoticed by those affected or at least not perceived as disturbing for a long time, as the addiction process is gradual. Internet addicts, as with other forms of addiction, become increasingly dependent on internet consumption to achieve a satisfactory emotional state. They thus try to deceive or reassure family members and other people close to them regarding the extent of their internet consumption. Parents should be concerned if: [20] [27]

- Usage time keeps increasing and other free time activities are neglected or even given up completely;
- Your child sits at the computer well into the night, is sleeping less, develops a shifted day-night rhythm, and is thus often tired during the day;
- Reacts very sensitively to attempts at limiting usage: moody, irritated or even furious when he or she has no internet/computer access or has to reduce internet/computer consumption;
- Vehemently negotiates about internet/computer consumption and/or secretly switches on the computer at night;
- There clearly are fewer actual social contacts, your child seeming to avoid any encounters, and discussions occur quickly and superficially;
- Your child neglects to carry out tasks and obligations (e.g., increased school absence, upcoming deadlines are postponed, often for weeks);
- Your child reacts in an irritated manner and an argument breaks out if you openly address the (addiction) problem.

If you have such experiences, you should take your concerns seriously, The ones affected often have great difficulty in realistically estimating their own internet usage, and thus need help from outside. Often feelings of shame in those affected are a reason for downplaying their own internet/computer usage.

Parental self-test for internet addiction
This is a list of questions for self-diagnosis: The questions were used by a Chinese team researching the effects of heavy internet usage on the brains of adolescents.[22][23]

1. Do you have the sense that you are completely immersed in the internet? Can you remember your last online activity, or are you longing for your next session?
2. Do you have a sense of satisfaction when you increase your time on the internet?
3. Have you been repeatedly unsuccessful in controlling, reducing or giving up your time on the internet?
4. Do you feel anxious, moody, depressed or sensitive when you try to reduce or give up your time on the internet?
5. Do you spend more time on the internet than you had originally intended?
6. Have you risked losing an important relationship, work, educational or career opportunity as a result of the internet?
7. Have you lied to family members, your therapist or other people to hide the truth about your internet usage?
8. Do you use the internet to escape from problems or to reduce anxiety conditions, e.g., the feelings of helplessness, guilt, anxiety or depression?

The researchers evaluate your answers in this way: "If you have answered 'yes' to questions 1 to 5 and at least one of the other questions, you have an internet addiction."

On the OASIS platform, sponsored by the German Federal Ministry of Health, you can do an online test for yourself or your relatives (for German speakers, have a go: www.onlinesucht-ambulanz.de/selbsttest). It is unique in that it offers additionally an online care service and can refer you to a relevant treatment center in your area. It is given here as a potential model for services in other countries.

With the search keywords "internet addiction test," you can find many self tests for computer game and internet addiction in English. Four examples are:

- **psychology-tools.com/test/internet-addiction-assessment**
- **psychcentral.com/quizzes/internet-addiction-quiz/**
- **www.ukat.co.uk/internet-addiction/**
- **www.screenagersmovie.com/internet-addiction** – a validated questionnaire for diagnosing problematic and pathological video game use, along with information and help links

The most important effects of excessive media usage
Lack of movement
Children who spend too much time in front of a screen often display delayed movement development. Too little movement leads to poor circulation, also in the head. This impairs fine motor skills, thinking, creativity, spontaneity and much more.

Excessive weight
People who spend more time in front of a screen usually are overweight. Excessive weight can have a series of serious consequences: diabetes (type II), arteriosclerosis, heart attack. The question is: Which is the chicken and which is the egg? Does too much television lead to excessive weight – or the converse? In New Zealand researchers observed 1,000 children from the time of birth until 30 years old.

The conclusion: Excessive weight, diabetes and also difficulties in school were in fact the results of high levels of television time.

Sleep disturbances
Many people fall asleep in front of the television. Does this mean that television promotes healthy sleep? For children especially the opposite is true: The more exciting a film or a computer game is, the worse a child sleeps afterward. Particularly if the television is on shortly before bedtime.

More time at the screen and therefore less time for sleep is also a disadvantage for learning: What is experienced during the day has to be processed and integrated at night.

Social contact and developmental disturbances
If, despite many virtual friends, hardly any real social contacts are nurtured, an important aspect of life is neglected. Relationship disturbances, developmental disturbances and increasing anxiety levels about life situations can result. Psycho-social maturity comes to a standstill, as time is lost for essential developmental steps.

South Korea is setting a good example!

Pediatricians in the USA have for years been warning about the above-mentioned risks and side-effects and have emphatically recommended that toddlers should not be given any digital media and that children should only have clearly limited times for using digital media. The South Korean educational policies have now applied these recommendations: South Korea is the first country in which the government, already since 2015, has put in place laws to protect the younger generation from the negative effects of new technology.

If you are under 19 years and buy a smartphone, it *has to have* software installed which
1. blocks access to violence and pornography,
2. registers the daily usage time of the smartphone and sends your parents a notification when you go over this time limit and
3. interrupts the connection to games servers after midnight.

The country with the most advanced technology has realized how important it is to protect the next generation from the risks and side-effects of these technologies. Worldwide South Korea is the country with the most advanced digital infrastructure and worldwide produces the most smartphones. As a result, in the age group of people from 10 to 19 years, 90% are already short-sighted, *over 30%* of children and adolescents have a *smartphone addiction*,[23] and many have postural damage because the cervical vertebrae are constantly in a bent position.

What is important?

Many parents are unsure about internet usage for their children. The intensive use of digital media in many families leads to arguments – all the way to illness and dependency. The earliest possible introduction to media purely to gain mastery over the technology is obviously not an adequate reason for independent usage and cannot be the sole goal. (Operational-) technical know-how does not safeguard against addiction. As a prevention this guidebook recommends that exposure to screen media is delayed for as long as possible and, instead, various alternatives from the real world are provided, which can provide a counterbalance for your child.

If it's "ablaze" and nothing can be done anymore...
If your child shows signs of addictive behavior, we recommend intervention at a counselling or treatment center. Some centers include:
- UK Addiction Treatment Centers: www.ukat.co.uk/internet-addiction. Their website includes a helpline number, a listing of centers and a self-test for internet addiction.
- The Priory Group in the UK: www.priorygroup.com/addiction-treatment/internet-addiction-treatment. The website includes an inquiry number as well as information on hospitals and centers which offer counselling or treatment.
- Restart in the USA: www.netaddictionrecovery.com. Their mission: "Sustainable digital media use for people and the planet." The nation's first center specializing in the treatment of problematic internet, video game and technology use.
- For a further listing of USA centers, see www.screenagersmovie.com/internet-addiction
- New Zealand: www.netaddiction.co.nz

Further information and help
- 7 Cups: a website which provides online therapy and free support to people experiencing emotional distress by connecting them with trained listeners. (www.7cups.com)
- An online search for "help for internet addiction," for other websites, as well as services and centers in other countries.
- www.familyfirst.nz

Suggested reading

Sherry Turkle (2018)
Alone Together: Why We Expect More from Technology and Less from Each Other, Basic Books

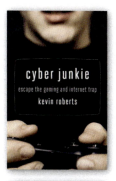

Kevin Roberts (2011)
Cyber Junkie: Escape the Gaming and Internet Trap, Hazelden Trade

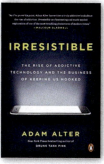

Adam Alter (2018)
Irresistible: The Rise of Addictive Technology and the Business of Keeping Us Hooked, Penguin

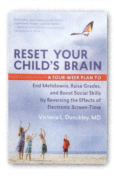

Victoria L Dunckley (2015)
Reset Your Child's Brain – A Four-week Plan to End Meltdowns, Raise Grades, and Boost Social Skills by Reversing the Effects of Electronic Screen-time, New World Library

7.3 Careless approach to private information

Ensuring the privacy of children and adolescents is very important: As a rule, you do not know to what extent your activities on a smartphone and the internet are open to unknown third parties and how much private information gets into their hands – either by using WhatsApp, SnapChat, Facebook, Instagram, Amazon, etc., or even when researching on the internet, e.g., with the search engine Google.

"I have nothing to hide!" – Really? What your data on the internet, smartphone or tablet betray about you
If you use the internet a lot – which is what almost all adolescents do – and thus reveal all manner of things about yourself, you are allowing your privacy to increasingly end up in the public sphere. Remember, the internet forgets nothing! Most search engines (e.g., Google or Microsoft) capture your searches and your IP address and use so-called tracking cookies which store your searches, the time of your visits, as well as the chosen links. Only a few search engines do not pursue you with advertisements or collect and distribute data about your searches (e.g., Startpage or DuckDuckGo). In the same way many websites save the links you choose and other personal data by means of cookies. Among the large search engines, Google has secretly compiled possibly the largest databank of personal information about individuals ever created.

Many apps – for example games such as Pokemon Go – have either hidden or even openly built-in spying functions. Around 60% of free apps require access to your address book, your location or GPS data, camera, etc., to function, even though this access often has nothing to do with the service offered and its only aim is to collect data.

> "Arguing that you do not care about the right to privacy because you have nothing to hide is no different than saying you don't care about free speech because you have nothing to say."

Edward Snowden

The data which inevitably arises when using the internet and/or smartphone with every click, is not only collected, but also compiled and, in many cases, automatically evaluated (with so-called algorithms) by many companies, such as Google, Facebook, Amazon, etc., and also by secret services: Your name, address, telephone number, birth date, gender, family circumstances, state of health, preferences, interests, political and religious convictions and attitudes, occupational and social status, social environment and cultural setting. But also consumer habits, credit history, payment morale, credit worthiness and much more data about internet users are compiled. This personal data profile (the so-called "digital twin") is sold to marketing specialists, banks, insurance companies, human resources departments, employees of authorities and other interested parties, even to hackers and criminals. So billions are made in profit. One can say that personal data is the gold of the 21st century, because almost everyone has been made into a more or less valuable, saleable product. The use of apps and other internet applications that are free of charge, is thus "paid for" by means of your data – hopefully not as a result of careless acceptance of agreements, without which the app cannot be used.

You are always getting the short end of the stick: The value of the app which you are receiving for free has a lesser value than your data which you have given away with it.

Loss of privacy means curtailing your freedom
Being spied on without your permission, which represents a deliberate disregard for your privacy, is an injury to your constitutional legal right to have data protection and privacy. This is increasingly being lost the longer you continue to carelessly give away your data on the internet.

This loss of privacy demonstrably leads to manipulation, control and limitation of your freedom. Whoever knows so much about one person can easily control and manipulate that person – and this is already in process.

The goal of manipulation is, above all, your consumption. For example, advertisements are becoming increasingly tailor-made for consumers. Often an attempt is also made to manipulate your attitude (keyword: fake news). You can also be placed easily under pressure or persecuted.

Your future possibilities and those of your child can be limited if insurance companies, employers, and banks, and so forth, as a result of digital data evaluations no longer react in an unbiased manner. For example, certain services (such as insurance) would perhaps be granted only with conditions attached, or a job application is rejected for unknown reasons, or credit or air travel is refused. All of these can significantly limit personal freedom and opportunities. The internet/smartphone is not only an ideal data transmission device, therefore an ideal spy, but also a means for surveillance, control and manipulation. Peter Hensinger[25] writes:

"The data for one's own monitoring, which previously would have been permissible only in cases of criminal behavior, is now supplied by every smartphone user on a voluntary basis, and this is new. It is a freedom trap ... it upstages Orwell's *1984*. The Austrian Federal Chamber of Labor writes about this in a depressing study[26]:

'The described development and practices make it clear that a kind of surveillance society has become a reality in which the population is constantly being classified and sorted on the basis of personal data.'"

Protect yourself and your children from loss of privacy

Most people would never think of revealing their private life to strangers. On the internet this is not avoidable. The most important preventative measure – if possible – is to block access to private information, or limit it, or, at the least, not recklessly share or post private information (name, address, friends, family circumstances, private pictures, etc.) The less personal information is accessible, the less of a "target" inexperienced users are. Children and adolescents have to learn and understand why the protection of their own privacy is so important and then how this can be implemented in particular.

Tip: Children who are using WhatsApp, Facebook or other services on the internet should never use their own name, instead they should use a pseudonym. Children under the age of 13 are not allowed access to WhatsApp and Facebook (see page 74).

With smartphones and with many online services users can determine the boundaries and decide which data to give. Settings can usually be determined in the user profile. Young users should be very sparing with personal information and have their parents help them.

Social networks have a good memory! Once photos have been made public, it is difficult to control their dispersal and they cannot really be deleted, because deleted pictures/contents will still exist in another place as a copy – children and adolescents should think about this before making anything public! Other data, such as addresses and preferences are also not so easily forgotten by the net.

Fundamentally this means: The less personal information your child provides, the safer the usage is. Therefore, provide only the data which are really necessary!

Develop media usage rules together with your children and adolescents, combined with comprehensive explanations about typical dangers and problems, especially in posting or sharing pictures or videos on the internet. Make clear to children and adolescents that an image or video, once it has been posted on the net, quickly spreads and cannot be taken back or simply deleted – with many negative consequences.

- Before downloading a free app, decide whether you or your child really needs it.
- Invest a little money if you can get an app which does not spy on your personal data on your smartphone, PC or tablet.
- Use VPN software from a reliable provider, which makes personal data anonymous when using the internet (VPN=Virtual Private Network), especially when using public Wi-Fi connections.
- Use the various indications on the internet and in books on how you can protect your privacy (e.g., YouthSpark - online safety oriented to teenagers: www.microsoft.com/en-us/digital-skills/online-safety?activetab=protect-whats-important%3aprimaryr3, and suggested reading on page 112)

Suggested reading

Agnes Nairn (2015)
When Free Isn't – Business, Children and the Internet, European NGO Alliance for Child Safety Online (eNACSO). Available as a PDF document: agnesnairn.co.uk/policy_reports/free-isnt%20_040416Sm%20.pdf

Dr. Elizabeth Kilbey (2017)
Unplugged Parenting: How to Raise Happy, Healthy Children in the Digital Age, Headline Home

Nicholas Kardaras (2017)
Glow Kids: How Screen Addiction Is Hijacking Our Kids, and How to Break the Trance, St. Martin's Griffin
In chapter 1, "Invasion of the Glow Kids," page 8, Nicholas Kardaras, PhD, former clinical professor, describes his first encounter with a 16-year-old boy who exhibited "screen gaming-induced psychosis," or GTP = Game Transfer Phenomena. Recommended reading by the New Zealand editor of this book.

Internet:

Delaney Ruston MD (2019)
Teen Sexting – What are the Laws? Tech-Talk-Tuesday blog on 'Screenagers: Growing up in the Digital Age,' www.screenagersmovie.com/tech-talk-tuesdays/teen-sexting-what-are-the-laws

Test how well you are protecting your private data[28]

You or your child have taken one of the first steps in protecting your privacy when all the boxes on the right have been ticked.

		not true	not always true	usually true	true
1.	The screen lock on my smartphone is always active.	☐	☐	☐	☐
2.	I have a random number combination for my screen lock.	☐	☐	☐	☐
3.	I am aware that in public LAN networks anyone can read my activities.	☐	☐	☐	☐
4.	I always set the "save my password" in the settings of my internet browser on "off."	☐	☐	☐	☐
5.	In the website settings of my internet browser I have set the "location" of my smartphone on "blocked."	☐	☐	☐	☐
6.	I have set the camera or microphone in the website settings of my internet browser on "ask first."	☐	☐	☐	☐
7.	I am aware that WhatsApp saves my telephone number and other communication data (time, receiver, address book contents …) and gives it to Facebook.	☐	☐	☐	☐
8.	When installing an app I always read the agreement first before accepting it and installing the app.	☐	☐	☐	☐
9.	I decline to install an app if I do not know what the agreement means.	☐	☐	☐	☐
10.	I decline the installation of an app if I know that images, videos, addresses, messages or location data are saved and passed on.	☐	☐	☐	☐
11.	I always install the newest updates for my apps and my smartphone myself and check what has been changed.	☐	☐	☐	☐
12.	I know the risks when I download and install the apps from Google-Store or from third party providers.	☐	☐	☐	☐
13.	I am aware that nothing is "forgotten" in the internet. This means that pictures, videos and texts can never be deleted with certainty.	☐	☐	☐	☐
14.	I know that my (future) employer can look at the pictures, videos and texts which I have put on the internet.	☐	☐	☐	☐

Risk: "Sexting"

An especially dangerous situation arises when young girls (under pressure or voluntarily) send intimate photos of themselves or even nude pictures e.g., to their boyfriend or even post them on the web (so-called sexting). It is safest not to even take such photos with a smartphone, as some apps can access these pictures without one even being aware of it. And if such photos are taken, they should not be sent to anyone, not even to a best friend. What happens to those photos or videos if the friendship breaks up or friends become enemies? Once the pictures are sent, one no longer has control over their further use (not even in SnapChat where pictures are automatically deleted after a short time, because copies can be made before they are deleted). As a rule, they are spread on the internet within a very short time and often instigate exposure, humiliation and even blackmail. Often they are defamatory.

It may be possible to prosecute the people who have circulated the images; even class- and schoolmates can be held accountable and punishable by law (see section 7.4 about age of criminal responsibility in different countries). In the UK it is against the law for any child under the age of 18 to take, share, download or store an explicit image or video or message about themselves or a friend (see the NSPCC site at www.nspcc.org.uk/preventing-abuse/keeping-children-safe/sexting). In the USA the specific laws depend on the state you are in. (For a chart of state rules see www.screenagersmovie.com/tech-talk-tuesdays/teen-sexting-what-are-the-laws?rq=sexting.) In general, it is against the law to send or receive nude pictures Most countries have similar rules, with variations. Many have enacted specific legislation around sexting among those under 18 to prevent offenses from becoming a criminal record for life (unless repeated or more serious), emphasizing education for children, schools and parents.

Under the search keyword "sexting" there is a lot of information and help, also for specific laws which apply for your region.

Risk: "Chatting with strangers"

A further danger exists in the offers of contact from strangers, who – most often under pseudonyms – initially gain the confidence of children and then seduce or force them to carry out actions from which they are not able to extricate themselves without help.

Explain to your children about such propositions and enticements. Most advice emphasizes not raising fears in your child about "stranger danger" but rather raising awareness of the differences between real-life friends and virtual friends and the precautions needed when exchanging any information with virtual strangers.

- See Common Sense Media website, www.commonsensemedia.org/blog/the-facts-about-online-predators-every-parent-should-know
- See *Unplugged Parenting*, Dr. Elizabeth Kilbey, chapter 7 on 'Online risks and keeping children safe'
- or search for keywords "online predators"

Help for the prevention of and intervention in sexual abuse of children
- Child Exploitation Investigation Unit/ICE www.ice.gov/predator (USA)
- Nation Assault Telephone Hotline **800.656.HOPE (4673)**
- online.rainn.org (USA)
- Child Exploitation and Online Protection command: www.ceop.police.uk/safety-centre. For information and for reporting online sexual abuse (UK)
- NSPCC Children's Services: www.nspcc.org.uk/preventing-abuse/our-services/childrens-services. They offer contact helplines, including a child line specifically for those under 18. (UK)
- Get Safe Online: www.getsafeonline.org/safeguarding-children. Offers information and advice on all areas of online safety, including safeguarding childen. Provides further links and helpline numbers. (UK)
- Childline: www.childline.org.uk/info-advice/bullying-abuse-safety/online-mobile-safety. Offers advice and helplines. (UK)
- Internet Watch Foundation: www.iwf.org.uk. For anonymously and confidentially reporting child sexual abuse content and non-photographic child sexual abuse images. (UK)
- Netsafe: www.netsafe.org.nz, a website for general online safety for New Zealand, but also with valuable information across a number of subject areas including cyberstalking and online sexual harrassment. They offer a 7-day-a-week helpline for free and confidential help. (New Zealand)
- Do a search for keywords "prevention of child sexual abuse" or "child protection advice" for help sites and contacts in your country.

7.4 Cyberbullying and internet harassment

Cyberbullying
With digital forms of communication and social networks, it is easy to take images or video footage of people openly or secretly and to circulate these, or to insult people, to spread rumors about them, to intimidate them, and so forth. This cyberbullying is increasing in schools. Boys and girls are equally affected by this (approx. 28–33%). Bullying includes forms of (mostly subtle) violence such as exposure, defamation, derision, among others, of people over a long time period with the aim of social isolation.

If visible aggression and physical violence are in the foreground, then one speaks of (cyber) bullying. There, however, is not a clear distinction between the two forms.

Bullying has taken on a dimension on the internet which in quantity and scope goes far beyond anything known before. According to a survey of the German Federal Association of Digital Economy (Bundesverbandes Digitale Wirtschaft), 97% of all 18- to 24-year-olds consider cyberbullying to be a serious problem in their age group.[29]

There are legal considerations and consequences (see also chapter 8):
- In many countries, the secret photographing, filming or recording of people and the circulating of these recordings is a criminal offense. In Germany, statute § 201a StGB stipulates punishment for the violation of personal privacy by taking pictures. The unauthorized recording and/or distribution of images or film sequences, especially in protected spaces, can in itself be punished with a prison term of up to one year or a fine. The classroom is not such a protected space; however, a changing room or a toilet is.
- Portraits may be distributed or publically displayed only according to copyright law with the consent of the person depicted. Violations in Germany carry the same sentence as in § 201 StGB.
- Punches and kicks are also criminal offenses because they cause bodily injuries. Filming or photographing such scenes, and then showing or distributing them, even if you were not involved in the violence, is also punishable; the distribution of such photos causes considerable humiliation and damage to the victim.
- Downloading violent or pornographic photos or videos from the internet and distributing them is also a criminal act. Such crimes can be punished with imprisonment or a fine and the mobile phone can be confiscated by the police. These laws apply in the USA as well.

Fundamentally, we need to take into consideration the fact that criminal responsibility starts at an earlier age than many realize and differ from one country to the next. In Germany it is once the child has reached the age of 14 years; in the UK, Australia and New Zealand, it is already at 10 years. In the USA for federal crimes it is 11 years; at the state level 33 states set no minimum age. Cases, however, are generally tried in juvenile court when under 18 years; juvenile delinquency does not focus on punishment, but on parenting. First and foremost, attention should be paid to education and support.

What can you do?
On the Childline and other websites (see links at the end of this section) are numerous tips and recommendations for how to protect against cyberbullying and to help others who are experiencing it, including:
- Find out if anyone in your family is being subjected to cyberbullying; speak to this person and try to help them.
- If your children are affected, they should not respond directly to the insulting, compromising or threatening e-mails or SMSs; instead initially secure and save the evidence (images or data).

- Prevent recordings (images, videos, etc.) from being distributed any further; instead, ensure that they are deleted. Arrange the deletion at the network server.
- In serious cases you should report the matter to the police, because cyber-bullying may constitute a criminal offense.
- If you want to report a case to the police, document the bullying process for the report; for example, collect photos, videos, the insult, coercion or threat, as the case may be, as a screen shot or as a recording of a chat conversation.
- Report bullying on social networks to the social media provider, as they can block the account of the perpetrator.
- Safeguard personal data from Trojans and Spyware by means of good virus protection; bullying is often carried out using stolen identities.

Further information and advice
www.thecyberhelpline.com/guides/online-harassment, for information, with helpline for the UK
www.childline.org.uk/info-advice/bullying-abuse-safety/types-bullying/online-bullying, giving information and helplines (UK)
1800victims.org/crime-type/cyber-bullying for USA
cyberbullyhotline.com for USA
www.stopbullying.gov/cyberbullying/how-to-report for USA
www.cybersmile.org/advice-help/category/who-to-call. A list of telephone numbers to call in various countries, including UK, USA, Canada, Australia
www.screenagersmovie.com/antibullying-campaigns for a list of organizations, websites and campaigns based in the USA
https://kidshelpline.com.au/teens/issues/cyberbullying (USA)

Do a search with keywords "help for online bullying" for further help options in your country.

7.5 Sites on the net which are unsuitable for adolescents

Shocking content on the internet represents a further threat if your child – often involuntarily – is confronted with it: For example, such pictures may suddenly appear in one's profile by means of the sharing function on social media networks, or school friends share what they have found. Among sites on the net which are unsuitable for young people, first and foremost, are pornography, after that, depictions of violence and advertisements promoting self-harming (e.g., anorexia, bulimia) and religious fanaticism.

With unrestricted access to such sites, the risks for the psyche of children and adolescents are numerous and cannot be underestimated, as the following selection shows:

Sexual representations – pornography
"Two thirds of all male adolescents between 16 and 19 years consume pornography daily or weekly, with one in five watching pornography daily (Pastötter, Pryce, Drey, 2008). Almost half of all 11- to 13-year-old children have already seen pornographic images or films. In the case of 17-year-olds it is already 93% of boys and 80% of girls." (Dr. Sommer Study[35])

The Return Institute for Media Addiction in Germany (Fachstelle Mediensucht return) writes as follows:

"Pornography is not harmless. ... Numerous studies have shown the consumption of pornography endangers the ability to have relationships, promotes sexual violence and is potentially very addictive. Children and adolescents need help to be able to see through the effects of the consumption of pornography and to develop a knowledgeable attitude about it."

Pornography also often leads to anxiety and false expectations about love and sexuality. Sexual assault among underage children is increasing. Long-term studies demonstrate. The more frequently adolescents consume pornography, the more they separate sexuality from any relationship context and consider casual sex to be the norm. Youth Protection laws and filter software are important, but are not adequate for prevention. Additional information can be found in the suggested reading below.

Suggested reading

Ed Mayo and Agnes Nairn (2009)
Consumer Kids – How Big Business Is Grooming Our Children for Profit, Constable

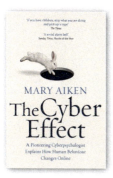

Mary Aiken (2016)
The Cyber Effect – A pioneering Cyberpsychologist explains how human behavior changes online, John Murray

Internet:

Child Safety Online – A practical guide for parents and carers whose children are using social media. A guidance leaflet produced by the UK Council for Child Internet Safety, assets.publishing.service.gov.uk/government/uploads/system/uploads/attachment_data/file/490001/Social_Media_Guidance_UKCCIS_Final_18122015.pdf

Screenagers movie. The official trailer for the powerful and informative film on digital device usage: www.youtube.com/watch?v=kJPdQaOQZho

The Impacts of Banning Advertising Directed at Children in Brazil (2017) The Economist Intelligence Unit. Available as a PDF document: agnesnairn.co.uk/policy_reports/eiu-alana-report-web-final.pdf

Campaign for a Commercial Free Childhood

Depictions of violence

12,000 hours in front of a screen. The "average child" in Germany has reached this count by about 15 years. According to estimates, a child has thus seen almost 10,000 murders and 100,000 acts of violence. Despite this, most adolescents do not behave violently. Especially the internet is filled with depictions of violence: videos of beatings, sequences from horror films, brutal advertising trailers, images of accidents, torture and even executions, and much more. According to the 2009 Grimm Study "Violence on the Web 2.0" (Gewalt im Web 2.0), a quarter of all adolescents have seen violence on the internet.[32]

What about headlines such as, "Killing sprees caused by shooting games on the PC"? There are many factors which protect adolescents from going on a rampage. Loving parents, good friends, a calm disposition, etc. However, there is also a lot which contributes to violence. A problematic circle of friends, violence in the home, stress at school. Media violence becomes an additional influence.

The effect of depictions of violence: breaking down empathy

Depictions of violence make a long-term impression on children and adolescents. They are shocked, experience revulsion, anxiety and uncertainty. The images can even elicit trauma. "Especially problematic are real and realistic depictions of violence, which more than 40% of adolescents have seen. They are dangerous because they have a greater effect on children and adolescents than on adults."

**Violence in the head?
– It is not that simple!**

The Grimm Study furthermore found: "In all groups, adolescents express outrage and incomprehension about the perpetrators and the acts depicted, and also about the people who film such things and distribute them on the internet. A critical attitude about usage of the relevant contents – and especially a critical attitude about their own usage of what is offered – is however expressed in only a few cases, it is especially the perpetrators and the people active in the production who are blamed."

Empathy especially is weakened by repeated viewing of violence. The ability to feel empathy decreases. This effect is even greater if one can "participate" in the events, as is the case in computer games or even more so in cyber games. The inborn inhibition to kill is weakened. If violent behavior were a car, then one would say: Media violence is not like putting high octane fuel in the tank, but rather that it damages the brakes.

Beware: Not every film or every game "from age 6" is suitable for 6-year-olds. Expert tip: USK/FSK + 3 years (see pages 66 and 73)

The manner in which representations of violence affect the psyche of children and adolescents is presented in more detail in the informative study, "The Influence of Media Violence on Youth" (Anderson, C.A. et al, Psychological Science in the Public Interest, 2003: journals.sagepub.com/doi/10.1111/j.1529-1006.2003.pspi_1433.x)

Self-harming

There are many sites on the internet that spread and often glorify self-harming and self-destructive behavior. Adolescents who are in danger and look for help on the internet for anorexia nervosa or bulimia nervosa, for example, are carelessly affirmed in their illness and even obtain tips on how to continue by so-called pro-ana or pro-mia sites. In Germany there are websites for reporting pro-ana or pro-mia pages (e.g., www.internet-beschwerdestelle.de). In light of the online hazards, people suffering from these conditions should exercise extreme caution when doing web searches to get help. They need urgent help for their mental illness. The references below are from reputable organizations and include helpline numbers. An important next step is to see a health professional.

- For information and a helpline about self-harming, see the NSPCC website: **www.nspcc.org.uk/preventing-abuse/keeping-children-safe/self-harm**
- For information and helpline for eating disorders, see the National Health Service (NHS) website: **www.nhs.uk/conditions/eating-disorders**
- **www.nationaleatingdisorders.org/help-support** (USA)
- **www.mentalhealthamerica.net/conditions/eating-disorders** (USA)
- **www.mentalhealthamerica.net/self-injury** (USA)
- **www.ed.org.nz** in New Zealand
- **thebutterflyfoundation.org.au** in Australia

What else you can do...

Technical protective measures, as described in Section 6.5, are not always adequate on their own to safeguard children and adolescents from content dangerous to young people.

Most important is a good relationship of trust, so that your child can turn to you when he or she encounters incriminatory experiences on the internet.

Encourage your children to inform you or the teachers at school if they come upon sites on the internet which are unsuitable for young people. Reassure them that they will not be punished if they have looked at such sites or have drawn in others too.

Show your children how political propaganda works and what dangers they submit themselves to through it. Children are often gullible and uncritically believe the messages depicted. Explain to them the meaning of the multi-faceted freedoms which we enjoy in a democracy, and that these are not guaranteed for all time.

Internet and the law

**Information
for parents**

CHAPTER 8 INTERNET AND THE LAW

With an increasing ability to judge, adolescents require precise explanations about why certain behaviors can have legal consequences. When adolescents learn to drive, so they can obtain a driver's licence at the age of 17 years, or whatever age applies in the country or state of residence, they are obviously familiarized with the road traffic laws. The internet also has such regulatory laws: There are general laws surrounding personal rights, the right to your own image, copyright laws, as well as criminal law.

Very few, however, know what consequences a simple click of the mouse can have or how to disentangle oneself from an undesired purchase agreement. In social media, pictures are circulated without any regard for the interests of the people involved.

The specific laws differ from country to country and in some cases from state to state within a country. In the USA, for instance, laws and policies on bullying and cyberbullying are different from state to state in scope as well as depth. In 2010 the US Department of Education developed a framework of 13 components within state laws on bullying, each state with a different mix and emphasis. (see www.stopbullying.gov/laws).

Laws and policies in relation to the dangers of digital media, as outlined in the last chapter, are also constantly changing and being added to in response to new concerns and campaigns. As illustration: In the UK, the government issued a consultative Green Paper in 2017 on Internet Safety Strategy, and in May 2018 issued a further Government Response anticipating the introduction of new laws "to tackle the internet's wild west," as described by the Culture Secretary, Matt Hancock. Up until this point, the UK, as does the USA, has relied more on industry codes of practice for many areas of internet safety, which the public increasingly believe don't go far enough.

In January 2019 the UK All Party Parliamentary Committee (APPC) on Social Media and Young People's Health and Wellbeing published a report in which it outlines four recommendations for actions:

1. A comprehensive digital education.
2. Development of guidelines for the public.
3. Establishment of a statutory duty of care and code of conduct. 80% of the public, in a poll commissioned by the APPC, advocated a tighter regulation of social media companies.
4. Formation of a new body to fund research, educational initiatives and clearer guidance for the public.

With this book we hope that readers may not only wait to see what develops over the years ahead but, from a more informed perspective, may be moved to help influence the course of actions taken, whether in laws formed on a national level or in policies adopted by the school your children attend, taking into consideration the developmental needs of children at their different ages.

This can be through writing letters to the respective persons, distributing books such as this, joining lobbying groups, and more. The ELIANT group (see list of partner organizations in the last section), for instance, has been instrumental in influencing EU legislation on digital education in schools to reflect childhood development. With joint effort, it is possible to shape the course of actions ahead, that they focus on children's health and well-being rather than on industry profits and interests, and that they adopt a precautionary approach where there are still question marks.

While the above on the one hand illustrates the changing scenes with regard to laws pertaining to the internet and the difficulty of one book or website giving an overview, it is nevertheless informative to have a snapshot of where laws are at the moment, for which we have chosen Germany as representative of an EU country and where this book was originally published. This snapshot will vary for each country, but many elements will apply to most countries. Some EU directives have helped unify laws across Europe, such as the GDPR (General Data Protection Legislation), and internet based companies such as Google and Facebook even if based in the USA, must follow GDPR rules for operations in European countries. Additionally, laws developed in one region often become models for other countries. It is hoped that the more detailed discussion below of German laws will therefore be an impetus for readers to become more familiar with the laws and guidelines that apply in their own region. Links and suggested readings in previous chapters have given pointers for helping in this research.

The text in sections 8.1 to 8.4 below is from the original German edition and was kindly provided by Stefan Feinauer, a lawyer based in Germany. A few reference notes for English information sources have been added.

8.1 The right of informational self-determination

The protection of personal data (e.g., email address, mobile number), also the right of your own image, is not an end in itself, but an essential part of the general law of personal rights (Allgemeinen Persönlickkeitsrechts, Art. 2 Abs. 1, 1 Abs. 1 GG). From this is derived the law of individual informational self-determination: This is the law which governs that you determine when and in which context personal life records are shared.

The legal definition of *"personal data"* is found in § 3 Federal Data Protection Act of Germany (Bundesdatenschutzgesetz). "Personal data" are so-called particulars that are personal or concern one's circumstances, or are about particular people or people who can be determined. These can be written records, but also photos, videos and sound recordings. If one makes unauthorized use of such personal data, in other words without permission (§ 4a BDSG) of the person affected, this is punishable (§§ 43, 44 BDSG). The affected person does not have to tolerate the use of his or her data without permission, but can, among other options, request the deletion of the illegally stored data.

Personal data – the raw material of the future?
It is furthermore important to emphasize again and again, that every visit on the internet leaves behind traces. "Personal data" is not described as the raw material of the future without reason. Even if one thinks that "one actually has nothing to hide," your personal data could have a high value for a third party. Examples of this are the lucrative trade of personal data and information or data misuse. An example of the latter is identity theft. In the best case scenario, you could be liable to pay for what someone else has ordered; in the worst case, you could unjustifiably be subjected to governmental surveillance measures. This is why even the preparation to spy out and capture data represents a criminal offense (§ 202c StGB).

In this context it is especially necessary to point out again the importance of safeguarding Wi-Fi connections, even if, based on the current legal status, one is no longer automatically liable if third parties – for example guests or friends – illegally download music, films or games. Useful links for Germany: www.klicksafe.de/themen/rechtsfragen-im-netz and www.irights.info.

8.2 Internet criminal law and the Youth Protection Act

Nowadays it is possible to find a wealth of information on the internet. However, it is not always possible to distinguish whether an opinion has been voiced or if facts are being discussed. The constitution considers freedom of speech to be of high value (Art. 5 Abs. 1 GG). However, this right is not limitless. One has to consider the interrelationship between the protection of honor and the constitutional right of freedom of speech. Spreading hate or propaganda for violence on the internet thus does not only violate the general interest, but also violates the rights of the individual and thus is a criminal offense (§ 130 StGB).

Very generally speaking: for the internet there are no exception regulations, the laws "of real life" apply here too. This is made clear by the legislation at various points in the relevant regulations.

For example, in § 184d StGB it is written that the person "distributing pornographic representations by means of radio, media or tele-services" is also punishable according to §§ 184 to 184c StGB (on the distribution of pornographic materials).

Youth Protection Act

In addition, the legislature has established the Youth Protection Act and the Youth Media Protection Treaty for the protection of children and adolescents from images of violence and pornographic content on the internet. Repeatedly chain letters are sent via social networks, threatening the recipient that a calamity will befall him if he does not forward this message to friends and acquainances. These messages and the forwarding of then can be considered punishable as coercion.

8.3   Copyright law

Copyright law protects artistic and scientific works with an artistic or original form of expression. Copyright protection law extends from the creation of a work and is independent of registration. This includes works such as photos, texts, music and film data. One is allowed to make a copy of copyrighted material for one's own "private use," however only if it is not in contravention of any copyright measures and the copy does not serve any "profit motive." Additionally, the work – for example, a music video – has to have been produced and published legally.

Uploads and downloads
If such works are offered for free on the internet, then one must, as the user, ensure that they are "automatically" copyright free. When downloading music files, in cases of doubt, one should inquire to the respective Performing Rights Organization, GEMA in Germany [see Wikipedia for a list of PROs worldwide: en.wikipedia.org/wiki/List_of_copyright_collection_societies]. Streaming services for movies which are offered free are, as a rule, illegal. If you, for example, upload a clip from a television series on YouTube, you are contravening copyright law and possibly are criminally culpable (§§ 106 ff. StGB). This law is all the more applicable if a copy protection on a DVD or other has been bypassed (§§ 95a StGB).

Personality rights
The "art copyright law" also protects particular personality rights, such as the right to one's own image. Every person has the constitutional right to determine whether he or she is photographed and how these photos are used, including distribution in public. The publication of photos on the internet which were taken at a disco-event, are thus fundamentally only publishable with the consent of the people depicted. Especially protected is private life: If someone without authorization takes photos of another person in a home and distributes them, thereby invading the highly private sphere of the depicted person, they are culpable according to § 201a StGB.

Helpful links concerning copyright
The most important information about copyright in Germany for parents can be found on the pages of www.internet-abc.de under www.t1p.de/8bd7.

References added for the English editions
For the UK the following pages are very informative: www.copyrightservice.co.uk/copyright/copyright www.copyrightservice.co.uk/copyright/copyright_myths

For the USA see: www.copyright.gov/help/faq
and en.m.wikipedia.org

Material copyrighted in one country may be protected in other countries depending on the international agreements. See www.copyright.gov/circs/circ38a.pdf

Kids Encyclopedia Facts has simplified explanations for children: kids.kiddle.co/Copyright

8.4 Purchase agreements and liability on the internet

Most adolescents have already downloaded music data or bought clothing and other items or participated in an internet auction. Very few will be aware that a resulting purchase agreement has arisen. The simple click of the mouse, as mentioned before, is sufficient for that.

Underage children (between the ages of 7 and 17) are legally competent in a limited sense (§ 106 BGB). But if they want to conclude a (purchase) agreement, the permission of their parents is required.

If an underage child, however, buys something with his or her pocket money (so-called "pocket money paragraph," § 110 BGB), the contract is valid from the start, because the allocation of pocket money is seen as the silent consent of the parents.

If an adolescent concludes such a contract on the internet, particular provisions apply for the protection of the consumer (§§ 312 c ff. BGB). According to the conditions specified in the law, one can disengage from a purchase by exercising the right of cancellation. No reason is required for this.

If an adolescent wishes to become a seller, he or she requires the consent of his or her parents. Consent is also required if the adolescent installs a homepage for commercial purposes. Irrespective of this, the liability risks contained in the Teleservices Act (Telemediengesetz) have to be observed. The adolescent as operator of the homepage therefore becomes a "service provider" and is thus liable for his or her own and also for foreign content. If there is a commentary function on the homepage or if contents are linked, then the adolescent is also liable for the content of third parties.

Conversely, caution is also required if the adolescent makes statements or comments on social networks, internet forums or blogs. Because, via § 7 of the Teleservices Act, the general laws again apply, for example the criminal code, the civil code, but also the Federal Data Protection Act and the Constitution. If the blog operator has no knowledge of illegal content, he or she is not responsible for it, and then it remains the responsibility of the adolescent who has made the relevant statements.

8.5 Legal obligations of parents

The district court in Bad Hersfeld on 15 May 2017 formulated the guidelines and duties of parents, should they allow their underage children to use a smartphone or WhatsApp (see www.t1p.de/bkqx). The parents thus have a fundamental "duty to provide parental supervision, control and avoid danger in the use of digital 'smart' media (smartphones, tablets, apps, messenger services), as well as clear agreements of media usage within the family."

Specifically, the following guidelines were formulated in the decision:

1. "If parents provide their underage child with digital 'smart' devices (e.g., smartphone) for continuous personal use, they are obliged to properly supervise the use of this device until the child reaches maturity.

2. If the parents themselves do not have sufficient knowledge of 'smart' technology and the world of digital media, then they have to acquire the necessary knowledge directly and continuously in order to properly fulfill their duties of supervision and monitoring.

3. There are no reasonable grounds for leaving a smartphone with a child at bedtime.

4. It is necessary to formulate a parent-child agreement regarding media usage in case of significant misconduct in the use of media by the child or by a parent, also if there is a danger of media addiction.

5. Anyone using the messenger service WhatsApp, in accordance with the technical specifications of the service, is continuously transmitting data in a clear-data form of all the contacts entered in their own smartphone address book to the company behind the service.

6. Anyone who, by using WhatsApp, allows this continuous transfer of data without first having obtained permission from their telephone contacts, is committing a criminal (punishable) offense in relation to these people and is thus in danger of being issued a warning with costs. (Note: see www.t1p.de/dma0)

7. If children or adolescents under the age of 18 years use the messenger service WhatsApp, the parents as custodians have the duty to inform the child about the dangers involved in the use of this messenger service and to take the necessary precautions in the interests of their child."

In the negotiated case, the guiding principles have been supplemented by specific conditions, which have to be proven in court, e.g.:

1. "The mother of the child is obliged to conclude a written *media usage agreement* with her son E. ...

2. The mother of the child is required to obtain *written permission* from all the persons currently stored in the contacts of her son E.'s smartphone, the telephone number(s) and the name – if so, in whichever form (pseudonym, abbreviation or first name and/or surname as clear data) – and that *the data* from there is regularly transmitted by means of the application used by E., namely WhatsApp, *to the operator WhatsApp in California/USA, where such data may be freely used for a variety of purposes by the operator under its terms of use.*

3. The mother of the child is obliged regularly – at least once a month – to have *discussions with her son* E. about the use of his smartphone and the contacts which are saved on it, and also to *personally inspect* the smartphone and its contacts. With regard to new persons added to the contacts

on the smartphone, the mother of the child then has to proceed without delay in accordance with the requirement under clause 2.

4. If the mother of the child ... cannot prove the existence of a written agreement in accordance with clause 2 with regard to all the persons listed in the contacts of her son's smartphone, she must *temporarily remove the WhatsApp application from her son's smartphone* and keep it off the phone until proof has been provided for all the people stored on the contacts.

5. The mother of the child is assigned to immediately collect her child's smartphone before going to bed and to provide him with an alarm that is not run on an online network.

Herewith the law, among other things, very clearly shows the extent of the duty of the parents to ensure that the personal data of uninvolved persons and their privacy are protected, and not jeopardized by the child's ignorant or careless behavior in the use of a smartphone. The gradually increasing loss of privacy is the greatest risk in the use of apps on smartphones and tablets. This is why the term "super bugging device" used for smartphones or for many apps is verifiable and justified.

Suggested Reading

Save Childhood Movement (2016).
Seven Priorities for Early Years Policymaking.
Available as a PDF document: www.savechildhood.net/wp-content/uploads/2016/10/Seven-Priorities-for-Early-Years-Policymaking.pdf

All-Party Parliamentary Group (2019).
Social Media and Young People's Mental Health and Wellbeing. Available as a PDF document: www.rsph.org.uk/uploads/assets/uploaded/8c1612c4-54aa-4b8d-8b61281f19fb6d86.pdf

All-Party Parliamentary Group (2018).
Mental Health in England, All-party Parliamentary Group on a Fit and Healthy Childhood. Available as a PDF document: royalpa.files.wordpress.com/2018/06/mh_report_june2018.pdf

Bibliography and References

Bibliography

Aiken, Mary (2016). **The Cyber Effect** – A pioneering cyberpsychologist explains how human behavior changes online, John Murray

All-party Parliamentary Group (2018). **Mental Health in England**, All-party Parliamentary Group on a Fit and Healthy Childhood, royalpa.files.wordpress.com/2018/06/mh_report_june2018.pdf

All-party Parliamentary Group (2019). **Social Media and Young People's Mental Health and Wellbeing**, www.rsph.org.uk/uploads/assets/uploaded/8c1612c4-54aa-4b8d-8b61281f19fb6d86.pdf

Alter, Adam (2018). **Irresistible**: The Rise of Addictive Technology and the Business of Keeping Us Hooked, Penguin

Carr, Nicholas (2010). **The Shallows** – how the internet is changing the way we think, read and remember, Atlantic Books

Children's Well-being in UK, Sweden and Spain: The Role of Inequality and Materialism, Ipsos MORI Social Research Institute in Partnership with Dr. Agnes Nairn (2011) agnesnairn.co.uk/policy_reports/child-well-being-report.pdf

Clement, Joe and Miles, Matt (2018). **Screen Schooled** – two veteran teachers expose how technology overuse is making our kids dumber, Black Inc.

Dunckley, Victoria L (2015). **Reset Your Child's Brain** – A four-week plan to end meltdowns, raise grades, and boost social skills by reversing the effects of electronic screen-time, New World Library

Ellyatt, W (2017). **Healthy and Happy** – Children's Wellbeing in the 2020s. Save Childhood Movement. Available as a PDF: www.savechildhood.net/wp-content/uploads/2017/11/Healthy-and-Happy-W-Ellyatt-Full-paper-2017-v2.pdf

Ellyatt, Wendy (2018). **Technology and the Future of Childhood**, Save Childhood Movement. Available as a PDF: www.savechildhood.net/wp-content/uploads/2017/11/DIGITAL-CHILDHOOD-Save-Childhood-Movement-1.pdf

EMF Academy (last update 7 February 2019). **9 Examples of EMF Radiation In Everyday Life (With Solutions),** emfacademy.com/emf-radiation-everyday-life/

Environmental Health Trust (last access March 2019).**10 Tips To Reduce Cell Phone Radiation,** ehtrust.org/take-actioneducate-yourself/10-things-you-can-do-to-reduce-the-cancer-risk-from-cell-phones

Experiences Build Brain Architecture, Harvard University Center on the Developing Child, video youtu.be/VNNsN9IJkws

Freed, Richard (2015). **Wired Child**: Reclaiming Childhood in a Digital Age, CreateSpace Independent Publishing Platform

Goodin, Tanya (2017). **OFF.** Your Digital Detox for a Better Life, Ilex Press

Greenfield, Susan (2014). **Mind Change** – How digital technologies are leaving their mark on our brains, Random House

Harvey-Zahra, Lou (2016). **Happy Child, Happy Home**: Conscious Parenting and Creative Discipline, Floris Books

Hensinger, Peter and Wilke, Isabel (2016). **Wireless Communication Technologies**: new study findings confirm risks of non-ionizing radiation, original German in magazine, Umwelt-medizin-gesellschaft 3/2016, available in English as PDF: ehtrust.org/wp-content/uploads/Hensinger-Wilke-2016.pdf

Hill, Katherine (2017). **Left to Their Own Devices?** Confident Parenting in a World of Screens, Muddy Pearl

Hofmann, Janell Burley (2014). **iRules**: What every tech-healthy family needs to know about selfies, sexting, gaming and growing up, Rodale Books

House, Richard (2011). **Too Much, Too Soon?** Hawthorn Press

The Impacts of Banning Advertising Directed at Children in Brazil (2017). The Economist Intelligence Unit. Available as a PDF: agnesnairn.co.uk/policy_reports/eiu-alana-report-web-final.pdf

Kabat-Zinn, Myla and Jon (2014). **Everyday Blessings**: Mindfulness for parents, Piatkus

Kardaras, Nicholas (2017). **Glow Kids**: How screen addiction is hijacking our kids, and how to break the trance, St. Martin's Griffin

Kilbey, Elizabeth (2017). **Unplugged Parenting**: How to Raise Happy, Healthy Children in the Digital Age, Headline Home

Kutscher, Martin L, MD (2016). **Digital Kids**, Jessica Kingsley Publishers

Manifesto for the Early Years: Putting Children First, Save Childhood Movement. Available as a PDF: www.savechildhood.net/wp-content/uploads/2016/10/PUTTING-CHILDREN-FIRST.pdf

Mayo, Ed and Nairn, Agnes (2009). **Consumer Kids** – How big business is grooming our children for profit, Constable

Mueller, Steve (last edit: March 31, 2017). **30 Days without Internet** – A Self-Experiment, www.planetofsuccess.com/blog/2012/30-days-without-internet-a-self-experiment

Nairn, Agnes (2015). **When Free Isn't** – Business, Children and the Internet. European NGO Alliance for Child Safety Online (eNACSO). Available as a PDF: agnesnairn.co.uk/policy_reports/free-isnt%20_040416Sm%20.pdf

Palmer, Sue (2006). **Toxic Childhood** – How the modern world is damaging our children and what we can do about it, Orion

Palmer, Sue (2016). **Upstart** – The case for raising the school starting age and providing what the under-sevens really need, Floris Books

Payne, Kim John (2010). **Simplicity Parenting**: Using the Extraordinary Power of Less to Raise Calmer, Happier and More Secure Kids, Ballantine Books

Pineault, Nicolas (2017). **The Non-Tinfoil Guide to EMFs**: How to Fix Our Stupid Use of Technology, CreateSpace Independent Publishing Platform

Price, Catherine (2018). **How to Break up with Your Phone**: The 30-Day Plan to Take Back Your Life, Trapeze

Protecting Your Children from EMF Radiation – The definitive guide, EMF Academy, emfacademy.com

Roberts, Kevin (2011). **Cyber Junkie**: Escape the Gaming and Internet Trap, Hazelden Trade

Ruston MD, Delaney (2018). **Groundbreaking Study Discovers an Association between Screen Time and Actual Brain Changes**, Tech-Talk-Tuesday blog on 'Screenagers: Growing up in the Digital Age,' www.screenagersmovie.com/tech-talk-tuesdays/groundbreaking-study-discovers-an-association-between-screen-time-and-actual-brain-changes

Ruston MD, Delaney (2019). **Screen-Free Zones** – How to Encourage More Face to Face Time, Tech-Talk-Tuesday blog on 'Screenagers: Growing up in the Digital Age,' www.screenagersmovie.com/tech-talk-tuesdays/screen-free-zones-how-to-encourage-more-face-to-face-time

Ruston MD, Delaney (2019). **Teen Sexting** – What are the Laws?, Tech-Talk-Tuesday blog on 'Screenagers: Growing up in the Digital Age,' www.screenagersmovie.com/tech-talk-tuesdays/teen-sexting-what-are-the-laws

Schoorel, Edmond (2016). **Managing Screen Time** – Raising balanced children in the digital age, Floris Books

Seven Priorities for Early Years Policymaking, Save Childhood Movement, www.savechildhood.net/wp-content/uploads/2016/10/Seven-Priorities-for-Early-Years-Policymaking.pdf

Sigman, Aric (2011). **Does not Compute: Revisited** – Screen Technology in Early Years Education, chapter in Too Much, Too Soon? (2011), edited by Richard House, Hawthorn Press

Sigman, Aric (2017). **The Downsides of Being Digitally Native**, Human Givens Journal, Vol 24, no. 2. Available as a PDF: eliant.eu/fileadmin/user_upload/de/pdf/Sigman.HGJ.2017.pdf

Sigman, Aric (2019). **A Movement for Movement** – Screen time, physical activity and sleep: a new integrated approach for children. Available as a PDF: www.api-play.org/wp-content/uploads/sites/4/2019/01/API-Report-A-Movement-for-Movement-A4FINALWeb.pdf

Sigman, Aric (2015). **Practically Minded**: The benefits and mechanisms associated with a practical skills-based curriculum. Available as a PDF: www.rmt.org/wp-content/uploads/2018/09/Practically-Minded-2015.pdf

Sigman, Aric (2005). **Remotely Controlled** – How television is damaging our lives, Vermilion

Social Media Addiction Should Be Seen as a Disease, MPs say, 18 March 2019, The Guardian www.theguardian.com/media/2019/mar/18/social-media-addiction-should-be-seen-as-disease-mps-say

Steiner Adair, Catherine Edd (2014). **The Big Disconnect**: Protecting Childhood and Family Relationships in the Digital Age, Harper Paperbacks

Turkle, Sherry (2015). **Reclaiming Conversation** – The Power of Talk in a Digital Age, Penguin Press

Turkle, Sherry (2018). **Alone Together**: Why We Expect More from Technology and Less from Each Other, Basic Books

Twenge, Jean M (2018). **iGen**: Why Today's Super-Connected Kids Are Growing Up Less Rebellious, More Tolerant, Less Happy – and Completely Unprepared for Adulthood – and What That Means for the Rest of Us, Atria books

References

[approximate English translations of German titles in brackets]

1. BLIKK-Medienstudie (2017). **Übermäßiger Medienkonsum gefährdet Gesundheit von Kindern und Jugendlichen** [Excessive media consumption endangers the health of children and adolescents]. Die Drogenbeauftragte der Bundesregierung.
    www.drogenbeauftragte.de unter www.t1p.de/81yt und: www.t-online.de unter www.t1p.de/aw80

2. Lembke, G and Leipner, I (2015). **Die Lüge der digitalen Bildung. Warum unsere Kinder das Lernen verlernen** [The lie of digital education. Why our children unlearn learning]. Redline-Verlag, München

3. **DAK-Gesundheitsreport** [DAK Health Report] 2007, 2013 u. a. www.dak.de unter www.t1p.de/b5q5

4. **Barmer GEK Arztreport** [Doctor's Report] 2012, 2013, 2016, 2017 u. a. www.barmer.de/presse/infothek/studien-und-reports/arztreporte, insb. www.barmer.de unter www.t1p.de/qy7m

5. www.bfs.de unter www.t1p.de/f3vt

6. Jing Wang, Hui Su, Wei Xie, ShengyuanYu (2017). **Mobile Phone Use and The Risk of Headache: A Systematic Review and Meta-analysis of Cross-sectional Studies**. Scientific Report 2017, 10. www.doi.org/10.1038/s41598-017-12802-9

7. **Quelle und Genehmigung: Kinderbüro Steiermark**, www.kinderbuero.at

8. www.emfdata.org; insbesondere: Divan HA, Kheifets L, Obel C, Olsen J. (2008). **Prenatal and Postnatal Exposure to Cell Phone Use and Behavioral Problems in Children** Epidemiology 2008 Jul; 19(4): 523 529; www.ncbi.nlm.nih.gov/pubmed/18467962

9. Bleckmann, P (2012). **Medienmündig – wie unsere Kinder selbstbestimmt mit dem Bildschirm umgehen lernen** [Digital citizenship - how our children learn to handle screens confidently] Stuttgart: Klett-Cotta. Siehe auch: www.echt-dabei.de

10. miniKIM (2014). Kleinkinder und Medien. **Basisuntersuchung zum Medienumgang 2- bis 5-Jähriger in Deutschland** [Toddlers and digital media. Research on the media handling of 2- to 5-year-olds in Germany]. Medienpädagogischer Forschungsverbund Südwest (Hrsg.), Stuttgart. www.mpfs.de/studien/minikim-studie/2014

11. Projekt BLIKK-Medienstudie – Erste Ergebnisse (2015). **Kinder und Jugendliche in der digitalen Welt stärken** [First results of the BLIKK-Media project. Strengthening children and young people in the digital world]. www.drogenbeauftragte.de unter www.t1p.de/nvy8

12. Medienpädagogischer Forschungsverbund Südwest (MPFS) [Media Educational Research Association Southwest]. **Jim-Studie 2013, 2014 und 2017**. www.mpfs.de/studien/?tab=tab-18-1

13. Lembke, G (2016). **Digitales verdrängt Soziales – und schwächt Jugendliche**. Zur Veröffentlichung der JIM-Studie 2016 [Digital supplants social activity – and weakens teenagers. On the occasion of the publication of the JIM study 2016].
www.diagnose-funk.org/publikationen/artikel/detail?newsid=1146

14. Spitzer, M (2009). **Multitasking – Nein Danke!** [Multitasking – No thanks!] Nervenheilkunde 2009, Heft 12. www.medienverantwortung.de unter www.t1p.de/vlyw

15. Spitzer, M (2016). **Smart Sheriff gegen Smombies** [Smart sheriff against smombies]. Nervenheilkunde 2016, Heft 3. www.vfa-ev.de unter www.t1p.de/7sa9

16. Korte, M (2014). **Synapsenstärkung im neuronalen Dschungel. Lernen und Hirnforschung** [Synaptic strengthening in the neuronal jungle. Learning and brain research]. Südwestrundfunk SWR2 Aula, 06.07.2014

17. www.bitkom.org unter www.t1p.de/tn4j

18. aus: www.abendblatt.de unter www.t1p.de/v1gz

19. Konrath, S.H. (2011). **Changes in Dispositional Empathy in American College Students Over Time: A Meta-Analysis**. Pers Soc Psychol Rev May 2011, 15: 180-198, first published on August 5, 2010.

20. Internetsucht im Kinderzimmer. DAK-Studie (2015). **Elternbefragung zur Computernutzung bei 12- bis 17-Jährigen**. Für einen gesunden Umgang mit dem internet [Parent survey on computer use among 12- to 17-year-olds. For a healthy use of the internet].
www.dak.de unter www.t1p.de/oet4

21. www.dak.de unter www.t1p.de/alcq

22. www.diagnose-funk.org unter www.t1p.de/btz7

23. Kunczik, M and Zipfel, A (2010). **Computerspielsucht. Befunde der Forschung. Bericht für das Bundesministerium für Familie, Senioren, Frauen und Jugend** [Computer game addiction. Findings of the research Report for the Federal Ministry for Family Affairs, Old Age Persons, Women and Youth]

24. Spitzer, M (2016). **Smartphone-Sucht wird bagatellisiert** [Smartphone addiction is trivialized]. www.swr.de unter www.t1p.de/6d93
and: Smart Sheriff gegen Smombies. Nervenheilkunde 2016, Heft 3 (vgl. 15)

25. Hensinger, P (2017). **Trojanisches Pferd »Digitale Bildung«** – Auf dem Weg zur Konditionierungsanstalt in einer Schule ohne Lehrer [Trojan Horse »Digital Education« – On the way to a conditioning institute in a school without teachers]. pad-Verlag, Bergkamen. Zu beziehen bei: pad-Verlag, Am Schlehdorn 6, 59192 Bergkamen; pad-verlag@gmx.net.

26. Christl, W (2014). **Kommerzielle digitale Überwachung im Alltag** [Commercial digital surveillance in everyday life]. Studie im Auftrag der österreichischen Bundesarbeitskammer, Wien.

27. Farke, G (Hrsg.) (2007). **Eltern-Ratgeber bei Onlinesucht.** Schluss mit den Diskussionen über endlose PC-Zeiten [Parent's guide to online searches. Putting an end to discussions about endless PC times]. HSO e. V., www.onlinesucht.de

28. Alexander, A (2015). **Herausforderungen und Chancen der Datentransparenz für Schülerinnen und Schüler der Sekundarstufe** I – eine Studie. Wissenschaftliche Hausarbeit im Rahmen der Ersten

Staatsprüfung für das Lehramt an Realschulen [Challenges and opportunities of data transparency for secondary school students – a study. Scientific paper in the context of the first state examination for teaching at secondary schools]. Eingereicht bei der Pädagogischen Hochschule Heidelberg.

29. Umfrage des Bundesverbandes Digitale Wirtschaft (BVDW) (2017). **Internet-Mobbing wird als Problem unterschätzt** [Internet bullying is underestimated as a problem]. www.t1p.de/x3go

30. **Media Protect** e. V. www.medienratgeber-fuer-eltern.de

31. Brazelton, T B and Greenspan, S I (2002). **Die sieben Grundbedürfnisse von Kindern** [The seven basic needs of children]. Beltz Verlag, Weinheim, Basel

32. Grimm, P and Rhein, S (2009). **Gewalt im Web 2.0**: Der Umgang Jugendlicher mit gewalthaltigen Inhalten und Cyber-Mobbing sowie die rechtliche Einordnung der Problematik [Violence in the Web 2.0: The handling of violent content and cyber-bullying by young people and the legal classification of the problem], Institut für Medienwissenschaft und Content GmbH www.nlm.de/fileadmin/dateien/pdf/Grimm_Studie_Web_2.0.pdf

33. Saalfrank, K (2006). **Die Super Nanny**. Glückliche Kinder brauchen starke Eltern [The Super Nanny. Happy children need strong parents]. Goldmann Verlag, Munich

34. te Wildt, Bert (2015). **Digital Junkies**: Internetabhängigkeit und ihre Folgen für uns und unsere Kinder. Droemer Knaur, München

35. Dr. Sommer Studie 2009 von BRAVO, Bauer Media Group. Available as a PDF document in German (search for "BRAVO Dr. Sommer Studie 2009")

List of images

Title photo: Syda Productions / fotolia.de
Page 8/9 Photo: norndara / photocase.de
Page 11 Photo: Rina H. / photocase.de
Page 12 Photo: freeday / photocase.de
Page 14 Photo: altanaka / photocase.de
Page 17 Photo: Miss X / photocase.de
Page 18 Photo: Krauskopff / photocase.de
Page 21 Photo: southnorthernlights / photocase.de
Page 22 Photo: LBP / photocase.de
Page 25 Photo: greycoast / photocase.de
Page 27 Photo: deyangeorgiev / photocase.de
Page 28/29 Photo: southnorthernlights / photocase.de
Page 30 Photo: LBP / photocase.de
Page 32 Photo: southnorthernlights / photocase.de
Page 35 Photo: kallejipp / photocase.de
Page 36 Photo: xenia_gromak / photocase.de
Page 37 Photo: keepballin / photocase.de
Page 39 Photo: pollography / photocase.de
Page 40 Photo: greycoast / photocase.de
Page 42/43 Photo: jUliE:p / photocase.de
Page 44 Photo: jUliE:p / photocase.de
Page 47 Photo: grabba / photocase.de
Page 48 Photo: stm / photocase.de
Page 51 Photo: vanda lay / photocase.de
Page 52/53 Photo: silwan / photocase.de
Page 54 Photo: stm / photocase.de
Page 56 Photo: Bildersommer / photocase.de
Page 57 Photo: SirName / photocase.de
Page 58 Photo: LBP / photocase.de
Page 59 Photo: southnorthernlights / photocase.de
Page 60/61 Photo: as_seen / photocase.de
Page 62 Photo: Weigand / photocase.de
Page 65 Photo: criene / photocase.de
Page 67 Photo: manun / photocase.de
Page 68/69 Photo: przemekklos / photocase.de
Page 71 Photo: inkje / photocase.de

Page 72 Photo: giulietta73 / photocase.de
Page 75 Photo: REHvolution.de / photocase.de
Page 79 Photo: Tinvo / photocase.de
Page 81 Photo: davidpereiras / photocase.de
Page 82 Photo: inkje / photocase.de
Page 84/85 Photo: giulietta73 / photocase.de
Page 86 Photo: giulietta73 / photocase.de
Page 89 Photo: coralie / photocase.de
Page 90 Photo: Julian Hilligardt / photocase.de
Page 91 Photo: arthurbraunstein / photocase.de
Page 93 Photo: coscaron / photocase.de
Page 95 Photo: Armin Staudt / photocase.de
Page 97 Photo: 2Design / photocase.de
Page 99 Photo: Rike. / photocase.de
Page 100 Photo: simonthon.com / photocase.de
Page 102 Photo: Armin Staudt / photocase.de
Page 104 Photo: burandt / photocase.de
Page 105 Photo: 2Design / photocase.de
Page 107 Photo: przemekklos / photocase.de
Page 108 Photo: REHvolution.de / photocase.de
Page 113 Photo: REHvolution.de / photocase.de
Page 114 Photo: inkje / photocase.de
Page 117 Photo: Armin Staudt / photocase.de
Page 118 Photo: Simon86 / photocase.de
Page 120 Photo: Armin Staudt / photocase.de
Page 122 Photo: Armin Staudt / photocase.de
Page 123 Photo: daviles / photocase.de
Page 124/125 Photo: Antonio Recena / photocase.de
Page 127 Photo: Jonathan Schöps / photocase.de
Page 129 Photo: Antonio Recena / photocase.de
Page 131 Photo: complize / photocase.de
Page 132 Photo: javiindy / photocase.de
Page 135 Photo: kallejipp / photocase.de
Page 136/137 Photo: suze / photocase.de

Partners/Sponsors

- AG EMF im BUND-Arbeitskreis Immissionsschutz des BUND e. V.
  www.bund.net/ueber-uns/organisation/arbeitskreise/immissionsschutz

- BUND-Arbeitskreis Gesundheit des BUND e. V.
  www.bund.net/ueber-uns/organisation/arbeitskreise/gesundheit

- Bund der Freien Waldorfschulen e. V.
  www.waldorfschule.de

- Bündnis für Humane Bildung
  www.aufwach-s-en.de

- Diagnose-Funk – Umwelt- und Verbraucherorganisation zum Schutz vor elektromagnetischer Strahlung e. V. (Deutschland)
  www.diagnose-funk.de

- Allianz ELIANT – Europäische Allianz von Initiativen angewandter Anthroposophie
  www.eliant.eu

- EUROPAEM – Europäische Akademie für Umweltmedizin e. V.
  www.europaem.eu

- Kompetenzinitiative zum Schutz von Mensch, Umwelt und Demokratie e. V.
  www.kompetenzinitiative.net

- Media Protect e. V.
  www.medienratgeber-fuer-eltern.de

- neon – Prävention und Suchthilfe Rosenheim gemeinnützige Stiftungsgesellschaft mbH
  www.neon-rosenheim.de

- return – Fachstelle Mediensucht
  www.return-mediensucht.

- Stiftung für Kinder
  www.stiftung-fuer-kinder.de

- Verbraucherzentrale Südtirol
  www.consumer.bz.it/de

- Zeit ohne Netz: Eine Initiative der Handballakademie Bayern e. V.
  www.zeit-ohne-netz.de

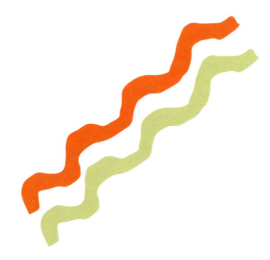

Important note
This book contains links to external websites of third parties over which we have no control. Therefore Waldorf Publications (publisher in the United States), InterActions (English publisher) and diagnose:media (original German publisher) are also not liable for this content. The provider or operator of the pages is always responsible for the content of the linked pages. The online links and suggested literature are given purely as indications for specific supportive material or further reading that is available related to the subject matter of the book and are not intended as endorsement of all the contents and pages of the book or website.

The information and advice in this guide were processed with great care by the authors and editors and were confirmed with media experts and educators. However, all readers have to decide for themselves to what extent they want to apply the suggestions in this book. In the case of health matters needing medical attention, they should not be taken as a substitute for seeking professional help. In this context, a warranty, liability or other legal responsibility of the authors or publishers for the content of this guide is precluded.

Note to the English translation and references
The numbered references throughout the text and listed in the back of the book are mostly referring to German documents and studies, with a few exceptions. As these were the basis for various findings noted in the writeup, they have been left in their original form, with English translations of titles put in brackets. On the other hand, for the Suggested Reading pages it seemed appropriate to find English titles on similar subjects as substitutes for the German books given in the original. This also applied to online sites referred to within the chapter texts, given as links for advice and further information. The readings and links may not be exact matches, and anyone wishing to see the originals please go to the website of the German publisher, www.diagnose-media.org, where copies of the German book may be ordered and where you can also find an online chapter-by-chapter edition.

Acknowledgments

Putting this book together in the original German edition was a collaborative effort of 15 organizations, spanning a period of over five years. It would be impossible to list all the individuals involved, including those who pulled all the research together for the final publication. We are grateful for all those who contributed to this process. A list of the 15 partner organizations is included in the back of the book. For the English edition I am indebted to Dr. Michaela Glöckler, a contributor and editor of the original publication, for her undying enthusiasm and support for getting the book to print in spite of very tight timelines. Further for this edition, we are grateful to the Ruskin Mill Educational Trust for their financial support for the translation; to Astrid Klee for the translation; to Gabriel Millar for the proofreading; to Chris Griffiths of StroudPrint for the layout work; and to Steve Goodall of Wynstones Press for his collaboration on distribution. Last but far from least I am grateful to my family for their patience while I kept my nose to the grindstone in order to meet deadlines, sometimes necessitating a temporary neglect of household duties. But the main inspiration through the process has been the book: as a valuable contribution to finding a healthy approach toward the use of digital media in childhood and adolescent years.

Richard Brinton
InterActions

We at Waldorf Publications add our gratitude to Richard Brinton's and state the honor and appreciation we feel at being able to publish this book for a North American audience, especially for Waldorf schools. We decidedly are riding on the coattails of the efforts of those who spent the five years described in the acknowledgments above. We most energetically thank Dr. Michaela Glöckler for her untiring focus on children, her striving to protect them from the contemporary and aggressive assault, largely from technology, on their well-being and their very childhood. This book is one significant element in this overarching work in Dr. Glöckler's assiduous efforts. We would also thank Richard Brinton for his patient inclusion of Waldorf Publications and our North American community in the receipt of the translated text and participation in the wider distribution of this good book through publication with us. Thanks, too, to Neil Carter in New Zealand. His edits assisted ours in making for a smooth manuscript in "American" English (not to be confused with the language of English used in the UK!).

Patrice Maynard
Waldorf Publications

Made in the USA
Columbia, SC
03 January 2020